CO-AMX-781

WESTERN EUROPEAN UNION

IMPLICATIONS FOR THE UNITED KINGDOM

University of
Illinois Library
at Urbana-Champaign

JUL 1 1 19

JUL 9 194

Return this book on or before A
Latest Date stamped below. A
charge is made on all overdue
books. University of Illinois Library

Jan 16 '51

JAN 16 1959

L161—H41

THE ROYAL INSTITUTE
OF INTERNATIONAL AFFAIRS
London: Chatham House, St James's Square, S.W.1
New York: 542 Fifth Avenue, New York 19

Toronto   Bombay
Melbourne   Wellington   Cape Town
OXFORD UNIVERSITY PRESS

WESTERN EUROPEAN UNION
IMPLICATIONS FOR THE UNITED KINGDOM

by
R. G. HAWTREY

*Price Professor of International Economics
at the Royal Institute of
International Affairs*

London & New York
ROYAL INSTITUTE OF INTERNATIONAL
AFFAIRS

The Royal Institute of International Affairs is an unofficial and non-political body, founded in 1920 to encourage and facilitate the scientific study of international questions. The Institute, as such, is precluded by the terms of its Royal Charter from expressing an opinion on any aspect of international affairs. Any opinions expressed in this publication are not, therefore, those of the Institute.

First published 1949

PRINTED IN GREAT BRITAIN
AT THE BROADWATER PRESS, WELWYN GARDEN CITY
HERTFORDSHIRE

341.1
H31w
cop. 2

SITTNER

Geng. 5 July 49 ned Diest 8 gly 49

CONTENTS

FOREWORD

IN February 1948 the Council of the Royal Institute of International Affairs convened a meeting of members to advise on a study of the implications of European Co-operation and of what Mr Bevin termed 'Western Union'. The general feeling of this meeting was that European Co-operation would grow out of the needs of the countries concerned. Those present thought that, with so wide a subject, the examination should initially be limited to the effect which a closer union of Western Europe might have upon the position and policies of the United Kingdom. This recommendation was adopted by the Council, and a study Group was set up under the Chairmanship of Mr Dingle Foot. The Group has held twenty-two meetings, some of which were attended by other specialists and experts.

The Group was as follows:

Dingle Foot (*Chairman*)
F. Ashton-Gwatkin
The Hon. F. D. L. Astor
Professor R. G. Hawtrey
Denis Healey
Professor Nicholas Mansergh
A. D. Marris
Lord Milverton
Sir Mark Turner

Mr Peter Cadogan was an original member of the Group, but was obliged to resign because of ill-health.

In September 1948 Mr Dingle Foot prepared a draft in which he epitomized both the differences of opinion on particular facets of the subject, and the substantial points of agreement. In November 1948 the Council accepted a suggestion from Mr Foot that Professor R. G. Hawtrey, a member of the Group, should be invited to prepare a report for publication. He has based his study on the material supplied by the discussions of the Group, but makes clear in his preface that the responsibility for what he has written throughout is his own, and not that of members of the Group.

This inquiry has been difficult, owing to the uncertainty of future international alignment. Though restricted in scope, the material in this book should be of help to all desiring to understand the practical points which have to be considered in giving effect to European Co-operation and Western Union.

The Council records its thanks to Mr Dingle Foot for his judicious and helpful conduct of the early proceedings, to the members of the Group, to the specialists, experts, and others who assisted, and to Professor Hawtrey for writing this study.

Those who read this study are reminded that the Royal Institute of International Affairs is precluded by its charter from expressing a point of view. The views expressed are not, therefore, attributable to the Institute any more than are the views which have been expressed by members of the Institute who have published works on this subject.

ASTOR
Chairman of the Council

CHATHAM HOUSE,
ST JAMES'S SQUARE,
LONDON, S.W.I.

AUTHOR'S PREFACE

THIS Study is the outcome of the appointment of a Study Group which was formed on the invitation of the Royal Institute of International Affairs in February 1948, to examine the implications of a closer union of Western Europe. A Group desiring to set out the results of its deliberations in a published volume has the choice of two alternatives: either to put together a set of separate papers, embodying from each member whatever contribution he is specially qualified to make; or to agree on a treatment of the subject as an undivided whole.

It was the latter course that the Group chose. But, even when discussion has revealed a high degree of agreement, it is not possible to obtain the concurrence of all the members in the contents of a volume, sentence by sentence. Inevitably, if the desired unity of treatment is to be secured, the writing must be entrusted to one *Rapporteur* or scribe.

That duty has fallen to my lot. But while no member of the Group is to be held responsible for any particular statements or opinions in the following pages, I wish to make clear that my task has been essentially to use the material which the Group's discussions have provided. I believe that at one time a new Speaker of the House of Commons would beg on his appointment that his merits be imputed to the House he represented, his faults to himself. The real substance of what this volume has to offer has been contributed by the combined efforts of the members of the Group. The scribe's duty has been to develop them in written shape, and I have done my best to fulfil it.

At the same time I may say that the Group was not primarily concerned to make recommendations for practical action, but rather to clarify a subject of vital importance on which there is much misconception on both sides of the Atlantic, and to give it dispassionate examination. Some advocates of union assume too easily that it is a step that can be taken without difficulty as soon as the word is given, and even that it would be practicable to make formal federation a condition of American aid. These are misconceptions which it is hoped that the deliberations of the Group can do something to dispel.

On recommendations for practical action there may be heated dispute, ending either in compromise or in dissenting opinions. But when a subject has to be explored, it is sufficient to bring out the considerations on which practical action would have to be based, and any positive assertion of what ought to be done can be dispensed with. Differences of opinion are chiefly on questions of emphasis.

Nevertheless where the discussions of the Group seemed to point to a definite position in regard to policy, I have preferred to state the upshot in that form, rather than adopt a balanced judgment, which would only have been a pretence. Even in such cases the responsibility for the statement is mine; the inference is not to be fathered upon the Group or any members of it.

I need hardly say that I have gladly made use of some of the written contributions of individual members of the Group. I have been able to lighten my task at several points by embodying them in the text.

R. G. HAWTREY

2 March 1949

INTRODUCTION

THE first premonitory symptoms of the rift which now divides
the West of Europe from the East appeared before the end of
1945, when the Soviet Union interposed to prevent the members
of the Polish Government which had been in exile in London
from assuming control of affairs on their return to Poland.
Thereby the attention of some of those concerned in projects of
research and study at Chatham House was turned to the question
of the means of co-operation between the countries of Europe
in the event of the Soviet Union deciding not to co-operate. The
question was not at that time ripe for systematic study. But the
breakdown of the London Conference two years later (December
1947) brought it once again into prominence.

By that time the economic co-operation of Western Europe
had become a practical political issue as a result of Mr Marshall's
offer of American aid in the reconstruction of Europe (5 June
1947) and of the Report of the Committee of European Economic
Co-operation, representing the sixteen nations which accepted
the offer (22 September 1947).

The decision of the Soviet Union not to co-operate had been
unmistakably registered in a refusal to accept American aid.
When the States of Eastern Europe under Russian influence
likewise refused the offer, the existence of a political barrier
dividing Europe into two groups was thrown into clear relief.
The barrier might not prevent bilateral arrangements for the
exchange of goods, but the plans for economic co-operation
between the nations which were then taking shape were necessarily confined to Western Europe.

For the Soviet Union and the Eastern European States who
had refused to co-operate had come to form a closely associated
group, welded together by Russian domination and communist
doctrine. Their union was as much political as economic. In the
political field grouping on one side leads to grouping on another.
European co-operation became the central theme of international
relations.

The immediate question at the end of 1947 was economic
co-operation. The idea underlying Mr Marshall's offer was that,

apart from the immediate issue of post-war rehabilitation in Europe, it was desirable on long-term grounds that the European economy should be more closely integrated, thus producing an economic unit comparable in size to the United States and U.S.S.R. But it was already clear that there were vital political aspects, and that, to be useful, a study would have to extend to the implications of European Co-operation, without limitation to the economic field.

Mr Bevin, in his speech of 22 January 1948 in the House of Commons, announced that the first steps were being taken to follow up the Treaty of Dunkirk for the mutual defence of Great Britain and France with a Treaty to include Belgium, Holland, and Luxemburg, and so to form 'an important nucleus in Western Europe' (a proposal soon to be realized in the Treaty of Brussels of 17 March 1948). 'We have then', Mr Bevin continued, 'to go beyond the circle of our immediate neighbours. We shall have to consider the question of associating other historic members of European civilization, including the new Italy, in this great conception.'

It was soon after this pronouncement that the Council of the Royal Institute of International Affairs invited us to form a Group with a view to producing a study for publication. The terms of reference proposed to the Group and accepted by them were to undertake 'An examination of the extent to which a closer union of Western Europe may affect the position and policies (economic, political, strategic and other) of the United Kingdom; the subject to be approached (i) from the economic standpoint in full recognition of the fact that the political and strategic aspects of the subject will immediately emerge for consideration; (ii) in the light of the immediate practical problems of the United Kingdom in the coming years'.

This reference did not cover all the problems of European union. It was confined to the position of the United Kingdom in relation to such a union. Which of the country's needs, present and future, would it help to meet, and how? And at what cost in new or increased burdens or difficulties? Would the military and economic contribution the United Kingdom would be called upon to make involve a net drain on her resources? And could the new commitments be reconciled with her position in the Commonwealth?

Part I
POLITICAL AND MILITARY CO-OPERATION

REASONS FOR CLOSER UNION

THE objects of the present movement for closer union of Western Europe are twofold, economic and military.

The economic condition of Europe in the spring of 1947 had become desperate. Measures had been taken during and immediately after the war to provide resources for the relief and rehabilitation of countries which were in need. The United Nations Relief and Rehabilitation Administration was provided with funds contributed internationally. For the special needs of Great Britain the United States and Canadian Governments made loans of large sums on generous terms.

But UNRRA was being wound up early in 1947, and the loans to Great Britain were being drawn upon more heavily than had been expected. The inadequacy of the provision that had been made for the recovery of Europe was becoming painfully apparent. And then the exceptionally hard winter of 1946–7 caused a strain on industry and transport, which at last culminated in an economic breakdown, not indeed prolonged, but serious enough to turn the scale against the progress of recovery. Progress had given place to regress. And, when there followed a disastrous drought, and a shortage of crops which threatened famine, Europe was seen to be sinking into an abyss.

The urgent need was for supplies from abroad. Imports were needed far beyond what the exports which Europe could spare would pay for. The trouble had the appearance of being summed up in an adverse balance of payments.

But the adverse balance is a *symptom* of an overall shortage of resources, the outcome not only of the ravages but of the burdens of war. War in the present century has become total war; the war effort makes a remorseless claim on all the resources of the combatant country. Not only is consumption cut down to the lowest level the people can be induced to stand, but the productive resources ordinarily devoted to the maintenance,

13

renewals, extensions and improvements of capital equipment and of property are diverted to war purposes. It is to this accumulated suspension of the services essential to the economic life of the community, even more than to the destruction directly caused by war, that the pressing needs of post-war Europe are due.

The shortage of resources so caused may be regarded as a *capital deficiency*, which, so long as it remains, gravely impairs the productive power of the countries affected. Industry and transport have to carry on with worn out, defective, or obsolete plant; workpeople are inadequately housed, clothed, and fed, and many of them have missed the training and experience which they would have received in quiet times.

Yet for reconstruction these countries must have a margin of productive power in excess of what is used for the consumers' current needs. They need a much bigger margin than under normal conditions, and yet it is only with difficulty that they can spare any margin at all. They are caught in a vicious circle: the impairment of production impedes the filling of the capital deficiency, and the continuance of the capital deficiency prevents the revival of production.

It is to provide a margin of resources for the restoration of their productive power that the countries of Western Europe need supplies from outside, supplies which they can only receive at the cost of incurring an excess of imports, that 'adverse balance' which is their nightmare preoccupation.

The industry of the United States has not been exempt from the strain of a gigantic war effort. But, great as the American war effort has been, it has never seriously impaired the country's productive power. The United States has a margin of such magnitude that it can spare something for Europe's needs.

Mr Marshall's offer of 5 June 1947 came at the moment of Europe's greatest straits. The offer was conditional on the recipient nations co-operating in a joint programme. European nations cannot become perpetual pensioners of the United States. There is a possibility that they may have to face a severe deterioration of their standard of living when American aid ceases. It may be therefore that their plans must look beyond a joint programme to a future economic co-operation designed to contribute permanently to the economic strength of Western Europe.

Co-operation of Western Europe in defence did not take shape as a practical issue till the breakdown of the London Conference of Foreign Ministers in December 1947. But, long before that occurrence, the divergence between the Soviet Union and her satellites on the one side, and the democratic nations on the other, had portended only too clearly the relapse of the world into power politics.

Communism had become militant. When the United States and other democratic nations became convinced that resistance must be offered to the spread of communism, the danger they feared was not merely a transition to collectivist institutions. For the communist parties of today aim at totalitarian rule, based on the forcible suppression of opposition parties and on subjection to Russian hegemony.

Economic distress and dislocation give the opportunity to the wrecking tactics of communist parties in those countries where they have a footing. And, wherever the presence or proximity of Russian forces overawes the political opponents of communism, it is only too easy for the communist party to place their nominees in the key posts of the Government, and then to extinguish all opposition by repressive methods.

As isolated units, the countries of Western Europe are exposed to being subjected one by one to militant communism. Nor can they feel any certainty that the pressure will stop short of direct military force. The remedy is to be looked for in mutual support, in such a degree of union for defence as will secure them against being taken in detail, and being overawed by Russian military force. In fact the purpose of co-operation of Western Europe in defence is to create a counterpoise to the military power of the Soviet Union and the communist group.

Even at the time of the Marshall offer in June 1947, Americans were alive to this situation. That offer was not directly related to the needs of defence, but it cannot be dissociated from them.

The offer was made to *all* Europe, including the Soviet Union. No country can afford to part with its resources gratuitously to a potential enemy. Was the offer to the Soviet Union inspired by the hope of killing militant communism by kindness? At any rate it failed, and thenceforward those nations that accepted the offer were marked out as potential friends or allies.

American aid was to succour their economic weakness.

Economic weakness means weakness in war. Western Europe, denuded of wealth, could make no stand against a threat of force. But if American aid was to contribute to the defensive strength of Western Europe, the nations accepting it must fulfil the indispensable condition of defensive strength: they must combine.

WHAT NATIONS MAY BE INCLUDED?

The two projects, economic co-operation and military co-operation, affect different countries in very different ways. Mr Marshall's offer had been to all Europe, but in consequence of the refusal of the Soviet Union and the satellite States of Eastern Europe, the programme of economic co-operation while including Italy, Austria, Western Germany, and Sweden, excluded all further East, except Greece and Turkey. Greece and Turkey were almost inevitably included, because material assistance was already being provided for them by the United States, on the grounds of their outstanding strategic importance and their exposure to attack—Greece in particular was endeavouring to cope with communist rebels who were receiving direct military support from neighbours under Russian influence.

Apart from Greece and Turkey, the participants in the European Recovery Programme were all the nations of Western Europe, with the single exception of Spain, which was (and is) looked at askance in consequence of the totalitarian origin and character of the existing dictatorship. The participants are endeavouring to give effect to the economic co-operation which was a condition of American aid. All have suffered from the war, but unequally; the neutrals, Switzerland, Sweden, Eire, Portugal, less than the belligerents. Denmark and Iceland underwent military occupation, but remained neutral. The eight who were belligerents have all (along with Western Germany) been severely hit. All except Great Britain have suffered from invasion and military occupation, and have come through the ordeal stripped of a great part of their resources, and with their finances and currencies disorganized.

Great Britain, defying invasion, yet had to sustain the heaviest economic burden of all. She had more to lose than others, and she had credit to draw upon which seemed inexhaustible, but which in the end was found to be pledged up to the hilt, if not deeper. Liberal and generous assistance from the United States and Canada maintained British fighting power during the struggle but with no margin.

Different as the economic circumstances of the nations of Western Europe are, all recognize the need of American aid and accept the condition of economic co-operation. On the other hand co-operation in defence is not so generally accepted. Yet, apart from the promptings of humanity, the principal ground for the grant of economic aid by the United States is a common interest in defence. While politically the two lines of approach to Western European Union, the economic and the military, have been quite distinct, they have a common root in the disabling effect of economic weakness upon European military power. Active warfare used up the resources of Great Britain. Enemy occupation and pillage depleted those of France, Belgium, the Netherlands, Norway, and Denmark. Defeat demolished the armaments of Western Germany, Italy, and Austria. The countries which remained neutral have never embarked on armaments on the grand scale, and they will prefer to remain neutral in the future if they can. American aid, with its corollary economic co-operation, is needed to restore the resisting power of a group of countries thus denuded of war potential. But whereas every country of Western Europe wants to see its economic life restored, it is not every country that is willing to assume military commitments.

A nucleus has already been brought into existence by the Brussels Treaty of March 1948, which binds the United Kingdom, France, Belgium, the Netherlands, and Luxemburg, each to afford 'all the military and other aid and assistance in their power' should any one of them 'be the object of an armed attack in Europe'. The Treaty is to remain in force for fifty years, and only thereafter is it open to any party to give a year's notice of denunciation. 'The High Contracting Parties may, by agreement, invite any other State to accede to the present Treaty, on conditions to be agreed between them and the State so invited.'

What other States are to be invited?

Of the sixteen participating in the European Recovery Programme, Greece, Turkey, and Iceland are not in Western Europe, and their defence problems have to be considered separately. Switzerland is unlikely to depart from her long established policy of neutrality unless very directly threatened. Portugal also is a special case. Her historically venerable alliance with England is still a living influence, but she is separated from the rest of Western Europe by Spain, and Spain is at present under a cloud.

Of the remaining eleven countries five are parties to the Brussels Treaty, three form the Scandinavian group, two, Italy and Austria, are converted enemies. There remains Eire, whose only enemy is her most intimate friend, the United Kingdom of Great Britain and Northern Ireland. Mr MacBride, speaking on the 20 July 1948 said, 'our sympathies lie clearly with Western Europe', but proceeded, 'the continuance of partition precludes us from taking our rightful place'.

The position of the Scandinavian group is one of increasing perplexity. To Sweden Russia has in the past been the hereditary enemy, and her fears and antipathies have been rather increased than diminished by the appearance of the Soviet Union in succession to the Tsar. Only Finland intervenes between Russian expansion and Sweden, and Finland, though she has not succumbed, is already in a very exposed and precarious position. On the other hand Sweden has by now maintained almost as long a record of neutrality as Switzerland. It is 135 years since a Swedish army was last engaged in warfare. The Swedes have every reason to be thankful for the preservation of their neutrality throughout the two World Wars of this century. And their present policy is to avoid commitments which would endanger that neutrality. Norway and Denmark, having had the experience of occupation by a totalitarian enemy, are less willing than Sweden to count on neutrality, and more willing to prepare armed resistance.

The three countries engaged in negotiations on the subject of joint Scandinavian defence in May 1948. The negotiations con tinued intermittently till January 1949, but failed to arrive at agreement. Sweden was prepared to conclude a defensive alliance to safeguard Scandinavian neutrality, provided the three countries kept aloof from other Western European military pacts. Norway on the other hand wished to remain free to participate in a Western defence system. Denmark endeavoured to find a middle course but without success. These negotiations became the occasion for a note of 29 January 1949 from the Soviet Union to Norway, attributing aggressive aims to the prospective Atlantic Union, contending that it would be outside the framework of the United Nations, and inquiring whether Norway was joining the Atlantic Union, or was about to allow air force or naval bases to be established on Norwegian territory.

The Norwegian Government replied that regional arrangements of the kind contemplated were in accordance with the purpose of the United Nations Charter when they aimed at preventing aggression, and gave an assurance that Norway would never co-operate in a policy with aggressive aims, and would not grant bases for armed forces of foreign Powers, so long as Norway was not attacked or subjected to threats of attack.

The Soviet Union replied with a note expressing dissatisfaction with the Norwegian reply, and inviting Norway to conclude a non-aggression pact.

This invitation, recalling the outcome of Finland's non-aggression pact with the Soviet Union, and indeed the almost self-evident fact that only an intending aggressor attaches significance to a non-aggression pact, was the cause of considerable misgiving. The episode has lent a new urgency to the question of Scandinavian participation in Western European union for defence.

There remain the ex-enemies Italy and Austria, and, more important than any, Western Germany. Austria, though she has her own government, is still subjected to military occupation, and her future position in regard to armaments cannot be settled in the absence of a peace treaty.

Italy's armaments are severely limited by the Peace Treaty, and the limitation applies to the manufacture of 'war material'. Nevertheless, as a partner in a military union, Italy could contribute man-power and an industrial war potential. Italian industry could be legitimately applied in peace time to the production of supplies and equipment which, though not 'war material', would yet be needed by the forces, and the adaptability of industry to the production of war material could be kept in view. Whatever the future of Italy's armaments, actual or potential, may be, the political and strategical importance of the country is very great, and the need to obtain Italian co-operation is recognized by the Powers interested in forming a Western European Union.

THE GERMAN PROBLEM

In the case of Western Germany the limitation of armaments is reinforced with more specific restrictions on industry. But there is no Peace Treaty and there may never be one. In fact the limitation of German armaments is not an obligation of Germany to the four occupying Powers but an obligation of those Powers to one another—an obligation which may be expected to sit lightly on some of them. It is widely held on purely economic grounds that a Western European Union must include Western Germany. But a corollary of that view is that German industrial capacity must in certain respects be restored and even expanded. There is here an antinomy between the two conceptions of Western Germany: on the one hand as a partner whose resources are to be available for the common defence of Western Europe, on the other hand as a potential enemy whose aggressive action is still feared as a danger.

The prerequisite condition of international co-operation is mutual trust. Inherent in sovereignty is independence in defence; every sovereign State is a potential enemy of every other. The League of Nations embodied an attempt to end that state of things, by instituting a system of collective security, pledged to come to the support of any member threatened by an aggressor. If the power of the League had been sufficient to over-awe all possible aggressors, nations could have ceased to regard one another as potential enemies, and could have co-operated in all affairs, economic and other, without considering the consequences to their relative power in warfare. The League never attained that ideal. It never included all Great Powers. The Great Powers within its membership were not all free from aggressive intentions, and the power of the League was never sufficient to over-awe even one Great Power.

The successor to the League, the United Nations Organization, is an improvement upon it only in openly admitting its limitations. Its impotence in face of opposition by a Great Power is recognized by giving each of the Great Powers a veto on coercive action in its capacity as a permanent member of the Security

Council, but in any case the United Nations would be no more able than the League to over-awe a Great Power; an attempt to do so would pave the way to a major war in which the United Nations would engage as a military alliance.

The fact is that peace in present circumstances is not secured by a decisive preponderance of power on the side of peace-loving nations, the world has reverted to power politics, and peace depends on a balance of power. Western Europe is looking for a counterpoise to the power of the Soviet Union and its retinue of communist States. Only in united preparation and action can a sufficient concentration of power be realized.

A Grand Alliance of threatened European nations, far from being a new departure, is the logical development of traditional British policy. Mr Bevin, when speaking in the House of Commons on 22 January 1948, still upheld Four-Power co-operation as the aim of British policy, and wished that 'the old-fashioned conception of the balance of power as an aim should be discarded if possible'. But he laid down as his first principle that 'no one nation should dominate Europe'. 'His Majesty's Government', he said, 'cannot agree to Four-Power co-operation while one of those four Powers proceeds to impose its political and economic system on the smaller States.'

It is as a more firmly welded Grand Alliance that Western European Union is to be envisaged. But the paramount requisite of a Grand Alliance is that the allied nations sink their differences. If Western European Union is to be a permanency, differences must be eliminated once and for all. That applies to economic as well as to military co-operation. National exclusiveness in economic policy has its root in power politics. A sovereign Power is unwilling to make concessions which would add to the power of a potential enemy. Whole-hearted economic co-operation requires that the nations co-operating cease to regard one another as potential enemies. Only so can united action become a reality.

The outstanding cause of difference in Western Europe is fear of Germany. At the present time a government of Western Germany is in course of being evolved. It is to be democratic in character, and capable, if admitted to a Union, of taking its place in a body representing the partners. To form a Western European Union excluding Germany altogether is an alternative hardly to be taken seriously. Conditions precluding rearmament will, no doubt, be imposed on the Western German Government, and, when Military Government ceases, military occupation will continue, along with suitable powers of inspection, to ensure observance of the conditions. But if the balance of power is ever to be tested by a conflict, it is not to be expected that German resources will be engaged on neither side, or that German territory will be kept neutral.

Even apart from the danger of Germany seizing the opportunity to ally herself with the enemies of the West, the defensive power of a Western European Union without German resources might be found lamentably inadequate. The five signatories of the Treaty of Brussels have a total population of 108 millions. The accession of Italy would add 47 millions. The Scandinavian countries and Austria might raise the total to 175 millions. But Great Britain alone has had the experience of adapting all its resources (indeed more than all) unreservedly to the needs of total war. The others either were neutral in the second World War, or were prevented by enemy occupation from thus developing their resources. The Germans endeavoured to extract what they could by pressure, but they met with a very limited and reluctant response, and nothing like a thorough organization of the industries of the occupied countries for war resulted.

Italy's armaments are subject to limitation by the Treaty of Peace, and in any case Italian industry has never possessed a war potential on the greatest scale. On the other hand, though Germany's war industries have been suppressed, there undoubtedly remains a vast potentiality of war production, which under present political conditions cannot be developed, but which cannot be left out of account in any calculations of the future balance of power. In the event of a World War, a disarmed Germany would offer these resources to whichever combatant was in a position to occupy German territory. It is obvious that a Western European Union cannot afford to surrender the industries of the Ruhr and Rhine valleys to hostile occupation; it must prepare to defend the territory which contains them.

Defence of a disarmed Germany by armies of occupation, in the semblance of a colonial dependency, is hardly a proposal to be entertained. An ally distrust of which is openly proclaimed and given concrete shape in enforced disarmament, is not likely to be reliable. Western Germany, if so treated, would surely welcome an invader who promised release from humiliation; it would be not merely occupied but armed, and would become a formidable support to his power. The Soviet Union would find it well worth while to make concessions to German irredentism in order to gain so powerful an accession of resources.

A union riven by distrust is no union. There is no escape from the conclusion that Western Germany must be admitted to a Western European Union on a footing of something like equality.

It is not practicable at the present time to sweep away the limitations on German armaments. The Soviet Union is still entitled to insist that the limitations on German armaments and war potential be maintained. And this remains a cardinal point of French policy. Nor has it by any means been abandoned either by British or by American policy, though the need for relaxations is beginning to be felt in both.

The Treaty of Brussels involves concerted plans of defence, in which the United States and Canada are to take part. Those plans inevitably presuppose decisions in regard to West German resources. And the pressure of facts is likewise felt on the economic side. The influx of refugee population has made Western Germany more deeply industrialized than ever. An economic policy which leaves the population permanently under-employed is out of the question. There is no opening for increased numbers on the land; Germany has long been a model of intensive agricultural development, and is probably near the limit at which more hands would mean less produce. Too rigid an exclusion of industries which would contribute to the war potential is likely to make the problem of employing German man-power insoluble. It would moreover obstruct the development of some of the forms of production most urgently needed to re-equip industry throughout Western Europe.

These great issues confront the statesmanship of the world.

To attempt to forecast how they will be solved would serve no useful purpose. But it does seem clear beyond dispute that Western European Union, if it is to be a reality, must include Western Germany as an independent nation, and not as a dependency.

POLITICAL INSTABILITY OF WESTERN EUROPE

The German problem is not the only source of weakness in the structure of a Western European Union. The project of co-operation in defence originated from the failure to reach agreement with the Soviet Union, and defence is understood to mean primarily defence against the forced spread of communism, with its corollary of totalitarian rule.

But communism is a powerful political movement in some of the countries of the West.

The defensive power created by the Treaty of Brussels depends on the combination of Great Britain and France. In the armaments of Great Britain an unequivocal priority belongs to sea-power and air-power. That is axiomatic. Only a residue of man-power and resources can be conceded to the land forces, and only a portion of that residue is available, after meeting the needs of home defence, for operations overseas. An attack calling for defence under the Treaty would have to be met mainly by the land forces of the Continental Allies, with a relatively modest contingent from Great Britain, but with powerful air support, both tactical and strategic.

Of those land forces the French would be the main part. The inclusion of Belgium and the Netherlands is important, because in the past their attitude of detachment and unpreparedness has been a fatal weakness in the defence of France. But France has more than double the man-power of these taken together. France also has the outlook and the experience of a great military Power.

France is at present a prey to political instability. Her troubles are for the moment due to monetary inflation and the resulting difficulty of adjusting wages to prices. But whatever the cause, democratic institutions are threatened on two sides: by the communists' hold on the more active trade unions, and by a not inconsiderable movement towards a dictatorship as the only effective retort to communism. Italy is at present outside the Treaty of Brussels. If included in a Western European Union, Italy would be an important source of man-power. But Italy has not the same long and great military tradition as France. And the political position of Italy is hardly less precarious than that of France. The establishment of a communist government in either France or Italy, or even of a dictatorship which, without being communist, was totalitarian, would wreck the prospect of Western European Union.

How can real union be possible so long as these possibilities have to be taken into account? How can there be unassailable mutual trust among the democratic nations of Europe if some of their number are liable not merely to abandon democracy, but to enlist in the forces of those who regard the destruction of democracy as the paramount aim of a class war to which they are pledged? These apprehensions do not presuppose a probability of a communist party securing the support of a majority of the French or Italian electorate and attaining power by constitutional means. The danger is rather in both countries that an active communist minority may gain power by wrecking tactics and entrench itself by methods of repression. Even if that is successfully prevented, and democratic institutions are preserved unimpaired, political instability means military weakness. A factious opposition may impede preparedness, and even in the ordeal of war disaffection may betray the forces in the fighting line itself. Its pressure may weaken the hand of the government in its conduct of foreign policy, especially by occasional temporary association with short-sighted or discontented sections of the people. It must be admitted therefore that there is no unassailable case for European union in defence. Union will be strength if it is real union, but not if it is a shallow pretence, hiding here an inextinguishable Franco-German feud, and there the threat of totalitarian government (communist or other) in France or Italy.

So it cannot be taken for granted that military co-operation with Western Europe will be on balance a real source of strength to the United Kingdom. The purpose of co-operation would be to guard against the countries of Western Europe being overpowered one by one. If the power of resistance developed in co-operation turned out in the end to be insufficient to preserve them from succumbing together, the United Kingdom would find itself after all isolated and, it may be, disastrously weakened by losses incurred in supporting the ineffectual resistance of the other partners.

France and Italy may live down their troubles, and a few years hence the resisting power of Western Europe may have become substantial and reliable. But it is fear of an *immediate*

25

danger which has prompted the movement towards Western European Union. And the question is whether an isolated Great Britain, with the backing which the Commonwealth can be relied on to give in a good cause, would not afford a stronger defence of democracy and of spiritual values than a combination with Western Europe.

The case for isolation cannot be ignored. But the choice with which statesmanship is confronted allows no room for compromise. If plans are to be made for the defence of Western Europe at the boundary which at present divides Germany, it must be possible to count on the concentration of adequate forces *in time*.

If the project of Western European Union were abandoned, the political consequences would be decisive. The same power which has over-awed the East would over-awe the West. The mere shadow portending the onrush of totalitarian repression would terrorize the supporters of democracy, and the substance of communist revolution would encounter little resistance. And the United States could hardly be expected to continue economic assistance to strengthen resources of nations on the point of joining the communist camp, and enlisting themselves in a class war in which the United States is regarded as the principal enemy.

It may be that a totalitarian communist Europe would stop short of making war upon either the Commonwealth or the United States. But the peace of the world would depend on a desperately precarious balance of power. In any case the prospect is one which political leaders in Western Europe, in Great Britain and in the United States would all alike refuse to contemplate. Policy is quite definitely set towards union.

PROPOSALS FOR WESTERN EUROPEAN UNION

The recent movement towards Western European Union has largely been inspired by the pronouncements of British political leaders and especially of Mr Churchill. Mr Churchill's proposal for union with France in June 1940 at a supreme crisis of the war, has already been accorded a place in history. More recently in his speech at Zurich on 19 September 1946, after referring to the imminent return of the Dark Ages, he went on to say:

Yet all the while there is a remedy which, if it were generally and spontaneously adopted by the great majority of people in many lands, would as if by a miracle transform the whole scene and would in a few years make all Europe, or the greater part of it, as free and as happy as Switzerland is to-day. What is this sovereign remedy? It is to re-create the European Family, or as much of it as we can, and to provide it with a structure under which it can dwell in peace, in safety, and in freedom. We must build a kind of United States of Europe. In this way only will hundreds of millions of toilers be able to regain the simple joys and hopes which make life worth living. The process is simple. All that is needed is the resolve of hundreds of millions of men and women to do right instead of wrong and to gain as their reward blessing instead of cursing.

Later he continued:

And why should there not be a European group which could give a sense of enlarged patriotism and common citizenship to the distracted peoples of this turbulent and mighty continent? And why should it not take its rightful place with other great groupings and help to shape the onward destinies of man?

Finally he concluded:

In this urgent work France and Germany must take the lead together. Great Britain, the British Commonwealth of Nations, mighty America, and, I trust, Soviet Russia—for then, indeed, all would be well—must be the friends and sponsors of the new Europe and must champion its right to live and shine.[1]

It is noteworthy that at that time Mr Churchill was contemplating a United States of Europe in which Great Britain would not participate. Great Britain and the Commonwealth were to be 'friends and sponsors of the new Europe', on the same footing as America and, if it might be, Soviet Russia.

Mr Bevin, in his speech on 22 January 1948, in the House of Commons, referred to above, said:

But surely all these developments which I have been describing point to the conclusion that the free nations of Western Europe must now draw closely together. How much these countries have in common. Our sacrifices in the war, our hatred of injustice and oppression, our Parliamentary democracy, our striving for economic

[1] *The Nineteenth Century*, Dec. 1946, Vol. CXL, No. 838, pp. 298, 301. The following note appears at the foot of this version of the Zurich speech: 'This address was imperfectly reported in the Press at the time. We give the full and authentic text with Mr Churchill's permission.'

rights and our conception and love of liberty, are common among us all. Our British approach, of which my Right Hon. Friend the Prime Minister spoke recently, is based on principles which also appeal deeply to the overwhelming mass of the peoples of Western Europe. I believe the time is ripe for a consolidation of Western Europe.[1]

He went on to say:

We are thinking now of Western Europe as a unit. The nations of Western Europe have already shown, at the Paris Conference dealing with the Marshall Plan, their capacity for working together, quickly and effectively. That is a good sign for the future. We shall do all we can to foster both the spirit and the machinery of co-operation.

On 5 May 1948 Mr Attlee stated:

I have often said that ultimately I believe we must come to a Federation of Europe. I have often spoken against the continuance of some absolute idea of sovereignty. The Motion is admirable in its general intentions, but suggests that things can be got over much more easily than is possible . . . As a matter of fact anyone entering into an alliance or treaty does take away to a certain extent their absolute power to do as they will. Therefore, in all these approaches, we do get a merger of authority, but to what extent we can go beyond that is a debatable question.[2]

The Hague 'Congress of Europe' of May 1948, in which Mr Churchill took a leading part, called for practical measures 'to bring about the necessary economic and political union of Europe'; declared that the time had come when the European nations must transfer and merge some portion of their sovereign rights so as to secure common political and economic action; affirmed the need of an economic union of Europe; and included among its ultimate objectives the unification of currencies and a full customs union, involving the abolition of all barriers to the movement of goods between all countries in the Union.

We are not concerned to criticize these pronouncements, but it is evident that they do no more than bring us to the threshold of our subject. At one extreme, Mr Attlee's statement, that every treaty involves some limitation of sovereignty, suggests that closer union might mean no more than a treaty on familiar lines.

[1] *House of Commons Debates*, 5th series, Vol. 446, cols 395, 397.
[2] *House of Commons Debates*, 5th series, Vol. 450.

At the other, the Hague Conference contemplated either a formal federation or something not far short of it.

There is a danger in giving currency to vague general notions without seeking to translate them into concrete terms, and without being clear as to how far Great Britain is able or willing to go in carrying them into effect. It is of the utmost importance that the British Government and British party leaders (who in this matter have a responsibility hardly less than that of Cabinet Ministers) should be clear in their own minds as to the extent to which they can participate in a Western European Union, and the conditions of such participation.

Promptings towards European union have also come from America, and recently they have become more insistent.

Mr Marshall, in his speech of 5 June 1947, started the movement towards economic co-operation by indicating, as a condition of further aid from the United States towards the recovery of Europe, that 'there must be some agreement among the countries of Europe as to the requirements of the situation, and the part these countries will take in order to give proper effect to whatever action might be undertaken . . . The role of this country should consist of friendly aid in the drafting of a European programme, and of later support of such a programme, so far as it may be practical for us to do so. The programme should be a joint one.'

But the American Administration were notably cautious in pursuing the matter. Mr Bevin's speech of 22 January 1948 was emphatically welcomed. The State Department itself issued a formal statement of approval: 'Mr Bevin has proposed measures which will enable the free countries of Western Europe further to concert with one another for their common safety and good. As in the case of the recovery programme, the United States heartily welcomes European initiative in this respect, and any proposal looking to a closer material and spiritual link between the Western European nations will serve to reinforce the efforts which our two countries have been making to lay the foundation for a firm peace.' (*Times*, 24 January 1948.) The State Department evidently thought it essential not to go beyond what Mr Bevin himself had advocated; any appearance of imposing political conditions on Europe had to be avoided.

Mr Marshall, who had just returned from Europe, where he

had been in close consultation with Mr Bevin, made a speech on the same day (22 January) as the latter (at Atlanta, Georgia). It was 'absolutely essential' to the ultimate success of E.R.P., he said, that the sixteen nations should go forward towards the European unity which they began in Paris in the summer. (*Manchester Guardian*, 23 January 1948). This was quite non-committal in respect of the nature and degree of unity in which the beginning was to find its development and end. But shortly afterwards (at Des Moines, 13 February) Mr Marshall was a little more specific: 'On the recent proposal of the British Foreign Minister, Mr Bevin, they have passed beyond their agreements for economic co-ordination to the consideration of a Western European Union. This development has been our great hope.' (*Christian Science Monitor*, 3 March 1948.)

Mr Dulles, who had accompanied Mr Marshall to London, having no official position, was free to express his own views without reservation. He had his opportunity when he appeared before the Senate Foreign Relations Committee on 20 January. 'There is need,' he said, 'of sufficient political unity, so that these states will present a solid front to any aggressor. The United Nations is not yet a strong enough reliance. So there might be a regional pact under Article 51 of the United Nations Charter, like our hemispheric pact made at Rio last year. So long as there is no regional unity for security, each nation will be weak and afraid' (*Hearings*, p. 588). He also thought there was 'vital need for some sort of a customs and monetary union between all, or groups, of the Western European States, including Germany'.

Mr Dewey, in a speech at Boston on 12 February urged that the aid to Europe be used to hasten some sort of European Federation. 'Aggressors do not attack nations they know are strong and united. Joined in a great federation, a free Europe can become a great bulwark for peace.' The Sixteen Nations have great material resources, but 'trade between them is hampered by national tariffs and monetary instability.' 'Can it be argued,' he asked, 'that we would be trying to force the nations of Europe into an unwelcome union?' Numerous pronouncements in favour of union from the nations themselves justified the answer, no. (*New York Times*, 13 February 1948). Mr Dewey and Mr Dulles both share some of the responsibility for the bipartisan foreign policy of the United States.

At the beginning of March when the Brussels Conference, which was to lead up to the Five Power Alliance, started its meetings, Mr Lovett of the State Department maintained official caution in regard to the possibility of the United States promising any support. 'We cannot put a roof on the house,' he said, 'until the house is at least partially built; we cannot decide what we will do until we know what those powers do at Brussels.' (*Christian Science Monitor*, 3 March 1948). But on the conclusion of the Treaty, the President himself described it as 'a notable step in the direction of unity in Europe for the protection and preservation of its civilization' and went on: 'this development deserves our full support. I am confident that the United States will, by appropriate means, extend to the free nations the support which the situation requires.'

The next step was taken by the Republican Senator Vandenberg, in pursuance of the bipartisan foreign policy. The Brussels Treaty created a regional pact within the terms of the United Nations Charter, and Senator Vandenberg obtained the approval of the Senate on 11 June to a series of resolutions which, designed generally to make the working of the Charter more effective, contained a recommendation for authorizing United States participation in such regional arrangements 'as are based on continuous and effective self-help and mutual aid, and as affect its national security'. That was not legislation, but an intimation of the views of the body exercising ultimate authority over the Treaty-making power. Ratification of a Treaty requires a two-thirds majority of the Senate, and the voting on the resolutions was 64 to 4. There quickly followed talks in Washington (6 July 1948) about possible military co-operation, in which Canada joined, and the project of a North Atlantic Regional Pact for defence against aggression began to take shape.

In pursuance of the Brussels Treaty periodical meetings of the foreign ministers of the five countries were to be held, and one of these meetings took place at the Hague on 19 July. On that occasion M. Bidault proposed the creation of a European Assembly representing the Parliaments of the five, and of other States wishing to participate. He also proposed a Customs Union of the five or of some of them. Mr Bevin and M. Spaak, while avowing that they did not object in principle, suggested that the five governments should study the proposals. And Mr Bevin was of opinion that they should be left to the private initiative of unofficial bodies.

From a correspondence between Mr Churchill and Mr Attlee, made public on 26 August 1948, it was learnt that the French Government had decided on 18 August to bring up the proposal again. But Mr Attlee in a letter of 21 August, adhered to the position previously taken by Mr Bevin.

The appearance of this correspondence provoked a protest from the United States. Mr McDermott, speaking for the State Department (27 August) declared: 'The United States Government strongly favours the progressively closer integration of the free nations of Western Europe. We believe that the world of today requires the taking of steps which before the war would have seemed to be beyond the range of practical politics. We favour the taking by the Europeans themselves of any steps which promote the idea of European unity, or which promote the study of practical measures, and the taking of such measures.' That was a pronouncement of the State Department, and was said to have been issued with the full approval of Mr Marshall, as indeed might in any case have been assumed.

This was, it seems, the first instance of any pressure from the American Government upon Western Europe to go faster. But whether the aim was to be interpreted to be a formal federation which would create a United States of Europe, or to be no more than a regional pact such as the United States had already concluded at Rio with the Republics of Latin America was left obscure.

At any rate the proposal for an assembly representing parliaments was revived by the French Government, this time with Belgian support. At the meeting of the Consultative Council (the five foreign ministers) on 25 and 26 October 1948, a Committee was appointed to report upon the steps to be taken towards securing a greater measure of unity between European countries. It was to consider the original proposal, along with a British counter-proposal for a European Council appointed by and responsible to the Governments, for the purpose of dealing with matters of common concern, and also any other suggestions put forward by Governments or by private organizations.

The British Government were prepared to accept the creation, alongside an authoritative ministerial council, of a consultative assembly, provided defence were excluded from its purview, but they wanted the members to be appointed by Governments and each country's representation to vote as a unit. The Committee failed to arrive at agreement on these lines, but the Consultative Council itself, meeting on 28 January 1949, adopted a proposal under which there would be, for matters other than defence, a Council of Europe, consisting of a ministerial committee, meeting in private, and a consultative assembly, meeting in public.

The proposal has still to be worked out in detail, but it is understood that each government will be free to select its representatives in the consultative body in the manner suited to its own constitutional usage. A country's representatives would vote not as a unit but as individuals.

Defence will be excluded from the consultative body's discussions, and its agenda will be under the control of the Ministerial Committee, though it will be free to submit proposals for subjects of discussion to the latter. (*Times*, 29 January 1949.)

Other European countries are to be invited to take part in negotiations for the establishment of the Council of Europe.

The disagreement that had previously been apparent on this question had led to allegations in some quarters that the British were holding back, and retarding progress towards union. These allegations Mr Bevin emphatically denied in a speech on 25 January. 'I would regard it', he said, 'as the crowning event of my life to establish European unity on a sound, definite and progressive basis. What I want to avoid', he went on, 'is a mere talking shop for the passing of resolutions. What I want is a practical organism in Europe, in which we shall cease to be English and French, cease to be English and Italian, cease to be English and Belgian, but will be European, an organism that can carry out European policy in the face of the new development of the world.' (*Manchester Guardian*, 26 January 1949.)

President Truman in his inaugural address on 20 January 1949 announced, 'we are working out with a number of other countries a joint agreement designed to strengthen the security of the North Atlantic area'. And the State Department had already (on 14 January) issued a full statement of the position of the United States in the matter.

The statement declared that the Vandenberg Resolution of 11 June 1948, referred to above, was not directed against any country or group of countries, but only against aggression. Treaties or appropriations arising out of it would be subject to constitutional process. The purpose of the steps that were being taken pursuant to the Resolution was not only to deter aggression anywhere in the world, but 'to reassure the free nations in their efforts to achieve security based on the recovery of their economic and political stability'.

The statement proceeded: 'the weight of an armament programme large enough to sustain even a minimum level of security probably would overburden the shaky economies of most European countries . . . It seems clear that the United States must supply much of the military equipment which the countries working for recovery cannot produce themselves. In so doing we must neither endanger our own economic or military strength nor deprive friendly nations of the aid we are providing through the recovery programme . . . What is needed is a carefully drawn balance in Europe between recovery and rearmament, and a similar balance here between the needs of our own domestic economy, our own defence, our contribution to the Economic Recovery Programme, and our contribution to European rearmament.

'The supply of military equipment alone to the friendly nations of Europe would only partially relieve their insecurity. . . Formal association of the United States with those countries in an arrangement directed against aggression evidently will be needed.'

Finally the statement referred to the conversations begun in July 1948 with the five nations of the Brussels Treaty and Canada, with a view to 'a collective security arrangement within the framework of the United Nations Charter, in which they and other nations in the North Atlantic Area might participate'.

PRONOUNCEMENTS FROM THE DOMINIONS

Here it is to be noted that the Dominions, with the exception of India, Pakistan, and Ceylon, whose attitude has been non-committal in public, have expressed a warm welcome for the steps already taken towards the consolidation of Western Europe. In particular the Brussels Pact has been warmly supported by all the older Dominions. In the Speech from the Throne in the New

Zealand Parliament on 22 June 1948 the Governor-General stated: 'My Government is confident that a closer economic, defensive, and spiritual union of the United Kingdom and Europe, which it regards as necessary and desirable, can be achieved without prejudicing the historic unity of the nations of the British Commonwealth.' When Mr Chifley visited Berlin in July, he said, 'No question arises where Australia stands. She stands with the Western Allies. Any other course would be unthinkable.' Dr Malan has stated that South Africa's policy is one of unyielding resistance to communist expansion, and his Government has indicated its support for the concept of Western Union, without indicating in any precise way what part in it they themselves might play in Europe. South Africa's desire to participate fully in plans for regional development *in Africa* has already been recorded.[1] Canada has gone further than any Dominion, in that she has joined the Western Union Defence Talks as a member of the Permanent Military Committee in London. 'The peoples of all free nations', said Mr St Laurent, 'may be assured that Canada will play her full part in building up an effective system of collective security by the development of regional pacts under the Charter of the United Nations.'

Again in September Mr St Laurent declared that the Canadian Government, anxious to bring all the freedom-loving nations into agreement to act together, had been urging at home and abroad, in public statements, and through diplomatic channels the immediate establishment of a North Atlantic security system comprising the United Kingdom, the United States, Canada, and the free countries of Western Europe. He believed that such an agreement would create the necessary preponderance of defensive force over any possible aggressors. For this reason Canadian participation both in the building up of Western Union and in the negotiation of a wider Atlantic Pact has been continuous and active. This statement of the Canadian attitude has a wider application, for the Dominions, other than South Africa, are concerned that any regional pact in Western Europe should be reconciled with the wider concept of the United Nations. It is for this reason that they tend to look upon the

[1] Speech by Dr D. F. Malan in the House of Assembly, 1 September 1948. (*The Times*, 2 September 1948.)

consolidation of Western Europe as a step towards a Security League composed of all free peoples rather than as a step towards the creation of a third great Power group.

On this point the communiqué issued at the end of the Commonwealth Prime Ministers' Meeting in October 1948 is particularly instructive. There, the Commonwealth Governments recorded their determination to build up the economic strength of their countries and to take all appropriate measures 'to deter and resist aggression; their general agreement that the association of the United Kingdom with her European neighbours under the Brussels Treaty was in accordance "with the interests of the other Members of the Commonwealth, the United Nations and the promotion of world peace"; and their desire that they should be kept in close touch with the progress of co-operation in Western Europe.'

It is to be noted that the Asian Dominions were represented at the meeting, and their views are presumably reflected, in common with those of the older Dominions, in the communiqué. But the communiqué does not go far to modify the non-committal attitude of the former.

While, therefore, it is essential that Britain's co-operation in Western Union should be so devised as to allow her a margin of resources and sufficient freedom of action to discharge her overseas responsibilities in Africa, in the Pacific, and elsewhere, the idea that there is any fundamental antagonism between her ties with the Commonwealth and closer union with Western Europe has little or no foundation. It is, however, true that Britain's ties with the Commonwealth rule out any rigid or theoretic approach to Western Union. With the steps that have already been taken for defence and economic recovery the Dominions, broadly speaking, are in fullest sympathy, but they would be inevitably disturbed by any indication that Britain was likely to become wholly absorbed in Europe. This is a factor which applies with most force to the Pacific Dominions. Therefore, anything in the nature of an actual federation would raise formidable and probably insurmountable problems (see below pp. 106-8).

The difficulties in the way of a formal federation of Western Europe regarded as an urgent matter of practical politics should not obscure the essential facts in the situation as it is today. The most important of these is that, broadly speaking, the Dominions have given their whole-hearted support to the concept of Western Union on the lines on which it is now developing. Their support means that the contribution which the United Kingdom can make towards economic and political recovery in Western Europe is all the greater. But the initiative and the responsibility for formulating policy in Western Europe lie with the United Kingdom. In deciding her policy this country's first aim must be to reconcile her interests in Europe and her interests overseas. That demands the very closest consultation at every stage with the members of the British Commonwealth of Nations. But responsibility is, and must continue to be, that of the United Kingdom.

EXISTING ORGANS OF CO-OPERATION

The two movements, one towards economic co-operation and the other towards co-operation in defence, have given rise each to its own organization.

The Committee of European Economic Co-operation, whose Report of 22 September 1947 was the immediate response to Mr Marshall's offer, recommended a joint organization 'to review progress achieved in the execution of the programme', and 'to ensure, to the fullest extent possible by joint action, the realization of the economic conditions necessary to enable the general objectives to which each country has pledged itself to be effectively achieved' (paragraph 113 of Report).

The European Recovery Programme was to be limited to four years, and the organization 'will be of a temporary character, and will cease to exist when the special assistance necessary for the recovery of Europe comes to an end'.

In pursuance of this recommendation the sixteen nations which had constituted the Committee concluded on 16 April 1948 (Cmd. 7388) a Convention setting up a 'continuing' (not a 'permanent') organization, the Organization for European Economic Co-operation (O.E.E.C.). A Council composed of all the members is the body from which all decisions derive. Members may be of ministerial standing, but need not be. Decisions (unless otherwise agreed for special cases) are taken by mutual agreement of all the members. If some abstain, 'declaring themselves not to be interested in the subject under discussion', the decision is none the less binding on those who agree. Besides taking decisions 'for implementation by Members', the Organization can make agreements not only with members but with non-member countries (including the United States) and international organizations, and can make recommendations.

Under the authority of the Council there are an Executive Committee (of seven designated annually by the Council) and such technical committees or other bodies as may be required. There are committees dealing with particular industries or groups of industries, such as coal or steel, chemicals, timber or textiles, or on aspects of economic activity, such as man-power, trade and payments, inland or maritime transport, co-ordination of programmes, etc. To serve the Organization, there are a Secretary-General and staff, who, 'having regard to the international character of the Organization . . . shall neither seek nor receive instructions from any of the Members or from any Government or authority external to the Organization'.

The Committee supplemented the Convention with Resolutions, the first of which defined the functions of the Organization more specifically. They are to include the preparation of general production, import and export programmes; consideration of the best use to be made of the productive capacity and man-power of the Members and their oversea territories; co-ordination of Members' purchasing policies; recommendations respecting the allocation of commodities; the most efficient use of external aid. The national estimates or programmes of development are the foundation of all, and the Organization is to promote mutual consultation and to create the machinery necessary for European economic co-operation, especially in matters of trade, international payments, and movement of labour.

The Treaty of Brussels also set up an organization: Article VII runs, 'for the purpose of consulting together on all the questions dealt with in the present Treaty, the High Contracting Parties will create a Consultative Council, which shall be so organized as to be able to exercise its functions continuously.

'The Council shall meet at such times as it shall deem fit', but, 'at the request of any of the High Contracting Parties, the Council shall be immediately convened in order to permit them to consult with regard to any situation which may constitute a threat to peace, in whatever area this threat should arise; with regard to the attitude to be adopted and the steps to be taken in case of a renewal by Germany of an aggressive policy; or with regard to any situation constituting a danger to economic stability'.

The Council consists of the five Foreign Ministers of the signatory countries, and meets every three months or oftener. It has a permanent organ in London, composed of a British representative from the Foreign Office, together with the diplomatic representatives of the other four countries assisted by a Secretariat. A Defence Committee under the Chairmanship of Lord Montgomery has been set up with its headquarters at Fontainebleau. It is politically subordinate to the five Defence Ministers, and an organ of mutual consultation, not of command.

The Treaty also provides for co-operation in economic, social, and cultural matters, to deal with which there are to be periodical meetings of Ministers or experts, and committees are to be set up.

These organizations are no more than a beginning. The Organization for European Economic Co-operation was originally conceived as a temporary expedient limited to the duration of the European Recovery Programme. But recently Mr Bevin has described it as 'not merely a committee for the Marshall Plan', but 'a continuing organization intended to go on after United States assistance had ended'. (*Times*, 26 January 1949.)

The Consultative Council under the Treaty of Brussels was regarded from the outset as a permanency: a fifty-year agreement with no provision for notice of termination is as permanent as anything in international affairs can be expected to be. But essentially it is a military alliance held together by apprehension of a common danger. A change of circumstances might change its character or lead to its disruption or voluntary dissolution. And it comprises but a small part of Western Europe.

Western European Union means something more than either of these. It means united action not limited to the transitory needs either of dealing with American economic assistance or of combining in a plan of defence. And the proposed European Council referred to above (p. 33) constitutes a step forward.

A FORMAL FEDERATION

The most ambitious and far-reaching plan of Western European Union is a formal federation: a United States of

Europe as closely knit as the United States of America.

The Organization for European Economic Co-operation, and the Consultative Council under the Treaty of Brussels both require unanimity. Those who have been engaged in concerting international action have had more than enough experience of what Lord Layton has called the 'Conference method': a meeting of representatives of Governments is held to draw up schemes or make recommendations, but with no power to bind their Governments; the matters agreed on come up for subsequent ratification, and each Government takes time to consider them; even if the recommendations are to come into operation as soon as a stated proportion of the ratifications have been obtained, it is left to each Government to take the requisite action, and too often the impetus towards action generated at the meeting has by that time been dissipated into nothing, and the measures taken, if any, are perfunctory and sterile.

Supporters of formal federation trace the fault, in the first place, to the need for unanimity, in the second, to action being the separate responsibility of the several Governments. Formal federation would entrust both decision and action to a federal authority with executive powers, overriding those of the several Governments in certain specified matters, and a federal legislature whose enactments would be directly binding on the inhabitants of the several States. In place of unanimity the legislature would arrive at its decisions by a suitable voting procedure, which would be binding on all. As soon as a matter became ripe for decision, it could be promptly settled one way or the other by vote. There might be dissatisfied minorities, and time might be spent in trying to satisfy them by suitable concession or compromise, but that occurs in the proceedings of a single State with a unitary constitution.

The federal executive would not be representative of the constituent States, but would be representative of their inhabitants as a body: either there would be a single head directly elected, as in the United States, or there would be a Cabinet jointly responsible to the representative legislature. Western Europe, being accustomed to the British type of parliamentary government, may be expected to choose the latter. Parliamentary government has not worked so perfectly in France, Italy, or Germany as to make this choice certain, but the experience of the directly elected executive in Latin America has not been encouraging in a world where an easy way to dictatorship would be a serious menace to liberty.

The legislature must be representative. It might be directly elected by the inhabitants of the federation, like the American House of Representatives. Representation in proportion to population, however, might cause some dissatisfaction. Every State large or small has its own specialized interests, specialized experience, and specialized wisdom; it is an organism, with something individual to contribute to the task of government. A small State may find itself with insufficient representation to make its voice heard, and, if the constituent States were not too unequal, the principle of one State one vote might be preferable. The inequalities in Western Europe are very great, however. It would hardly be defensible to give equal voting power to Great Britain, France or Italy, on one side, each with over forty million inhabitants, and to Luxemburg, on the other, with 300,000, or even to Norway with 3,100,000 or Holland with 9,600,000.

A compromise might be found in a voting power intermediate between equality and the population proportion, so that the number of electors to each representative in small States would be less than in large, yet not less in proportion to population. It would be desirable to adopt a definite formula for this purpose once and for all, otherwise with changing conditions every revision would involve a dispute.

Instead of a directly elected house of representatives, the federal legislature might be formed of delegates appointed by Governments. The problem of voting power could be dealt with in much the same way as with a directly elected assembly, but each delegation would vote as a unit. A third possibility would be the election of the representatives of each State by the State's own Parliament.

Supporters of federation would for the most part regard a directly elected body as essential to their aims, on the ground that the vitality of a federation depends on its having an organ directly reflecting the sentiments of individual electors, who can forget their party affiliations and parochial differences when they turn their attention to federal issues.

An assembly representative of Parliaments would be a tolerable makeshift in that it would be a body representing nations otherwise than through Governments, and could be brought into being without losing time in solving the many problems which would arise out of the creation of an international electorate. But it is likely to have the disadvantage of representing too faithfully the outlook of the existing political parties, and no doubt advocates of federation would regard it as a stepping stone to direct election. At the same time they would in general recognize the necessity of some organ directly representative of Governments. It might function as a second chamber of the legislature, like the American Senate or the German Bundesrath. Its procedure raises the same problems of voting power as that of the directly elected body, but they need not be solved in the same way. If the latter body adopted voting in proportion to population, the other might as a counterpoise give the States equal voting power, or voting power allocated by a formula.

Mr Lionel Curtis in his *World War, its Cause and Cure* (2nd edition, p. 80) has proposed that in a federation formed for purposes of defence or collective security, the financial contributions from the Member States should be proportioned to taxable capacity estimated (at intervals of five years) by a standing commission of financial experts, and that the same taxable capacity might be made the fundamental basis of representation and of relative voting power (p. 111). He was then discussing a project for forming a closer union of the British Commonwealth as the nucleus for a wider international union. As India had three-fourths of the population to be represented, a voting power proportioned to population could not be contemplated, and taxable capacity appeared to offer a way out of the difficulty. But the difficulty of arriving at any agreed formula for reckoning taxable capacity would be very great, and in any case there is no very strong presumption that (for a union which is not to include India) taxable capacity would give more acceptable results than population.

If union means union, it may be contended, then union means federation; an association of sovereign States, with no single authority possessing power to bind them, is but a concourse of atoms combining today and separating tomorrow. So long as they agree, they can co-operate, but the co-operation remains precarious while any dissentient is free to repudiate it.

That is an extreme view. When the need for co-operation is

recognized to be urgent, when the threat of a common enemy calls for union in defence, when economic problems seem insoluble without mutual support, continued co-operation may be better assured by the pressure of these needs than by any formal constitutional bond. Circumstances compel agreed decisions, which, once reached, give all the cohesive force that can be desired.

And federation, whatever its merits, cannot be established in any short time. A democratically governed country cannot commit itself to so great a change without obtaining support for it in principle, through a parliament elected after it has been recognized to be a practical issue. Elections held for such a purpose must be preceded by a preliminary educative period, to create an informed public opinion on the subject, and must be timed to suit the political situation in each country.

When the Governments of the countries to be federated have been duly fortified by democratic support, they can set up an organization representing them to grapple with the task of constitution making. This is likely to be a lengthy process. It involves not only the creation of the organs of federal government, the executive and legislature, but a definition of the powers to be conferred on these, and the setting up of a Federal Court with authority to decide whether particular acts of the federal executive or legislature or of any State executive or legislature are constitutional, in the sense of observing the limits so defined. There must be a written constitution, which will be in essence a treaty whereby the federating States agree with one another to surrender a defined portion of their sovereignty to the federal authority. Provision must be made for amending the constitution by some agreed procedure.

In all these matters there is room for wide differences of opinion, which, where they are serious, must be reconciled by persuasion and compromise if they are not to wreck the whole scheme. Federation is planned as a permanency. Even if the constitution allows secession, secession would mean failure. And the union may be so close that secession becomes impracticable, or at any rate involves a shattering economic, social, and political disruption. Whatever is proposed must be weighed and assessed by the peoples concerned as a permanent commitment. They cannot afford to cut short debate by the adoption of hasty and provisional expedients.

Experience of the creation of federal unions has shown that the practical problems arise not so much from any difficulty in formulating good democratic institutions as from the divergent characteristics, interests, and needs of the communities to be united. Even the thirteen Colonies which combined to form the United States, comparatively homogeneous though they were, encountered difficulties which delayed the adoption of a constitution for years.

The Government of India Act of 1935 contains nearly five hundred sections, and was the result of a long process of constitutional development and of seven years' intensive study and preparation. India was already under a single paramount Government, and the question at issue was not how to unify independent sovereignties, but how to reconcile the existing unity with the separate aspirations of the Provinces and States, and to substitute federal institutions for British rule. Yet the Act of 1935 was far from being a solution, and the grant of Indian independence revealed unsolved problems some of which still threaten a resort to violence.

Even for the five signatories of the Treaty of Brussels, the evolution of a federal constitution would at the best undoubtedly be a matter of years. The inclusion of Italy, the Scandinavian countries, Western Germany, Austria, or any others, would be a further complication. Therefore though advocates of federation may start feeling their way, and preparing the ground for the future realization of their hopes, they can in any case offer no immediate solution of the problem of united action.

In the face of the urgent tasks of the present time, neither political leaders nor members of parliaments can afford to give time and attention to the far-reaching issues involved in federal constitution making. For the time being the means of concerted action must be sought in a development of the agencies already in existence, the Consultative Council under the Treaty of Brussels, and the O.E.E.C.

Whether the measures to be taken in the near future should be conceived as steps leading up to a formal federation some years hence, or as instalments of an extended system of consultation and co-operation to be modelled on the present practice, is a question to be considered at a later stage, after the scope of the co-operation in prospect has been examined in detail (below pp. 101-8).

MILITARY CO-OPERATION

The problem of Western European Co-operation was brought into the present-day arena of practical politics in the first instance by the need for economic co-operation, and public attention was only directed after an interval to the need for co-operation in defence. Nevertheless it will be convenient, in order of treatment, to give precedence to defence, and to discuss it before the economic aspects. Military co-operation imposes limiting conditions on economic co-operation, and it is best to clear the ground by specifying those conditions before embarking on the complications of economic co-operation.

The forces of the co-operating countries must be under the direction of an authority so constituted that its decisions will not be seriously impeded, delayed, or frustrated by differences of opinion among them. A complete merger of armaments, leaving the co-operating countries without any armaments at their separate disposal (except possibly a local militia as a support for the police), would be inconsistent with any union less than formal federation. With the problems of formal federation we shall deal presently. We have now to turn to those of a co-operation in defence falling short of a merger of armaments.

The lowest level of co-operation is a military alliance of the traditional type, an agreement by all the Allies to combine in resisting an attack on any one of them, or an attack by certain specified enemies. To make such an alliance effective, the first requisite is consultation between staffs and agreement on joint plans in case of war. So much might be attained without interfering with the free discretion of each ally to determine the scale of its forces, of its preparations in time of peace, and of its effort in time of war. The plans would take all these as *given*.

Defence policy has several distinct aspects. A country has to form some idea of the contingencies it has to arm against, the enemies it may have to face and the character of a possible conflict with each. It must decide what proportion of its resources it is prepared to devote to defence. It must devise the best use of these resources, that is to say, the character of the armaments to which they are to be applied. It must construct and organize the desired armaments. Finally, it must make plans for the employment of the armaments in the conflicts to be provided against.

These different branches of defence policy are mutually dependent. The plans of campaign depend on the armaments available. The armaments to be provided will be determined by the uses to which they are to be put, subject to the limit imposed by the resources that can be applied. But the resources in turn will not be a rigid limit; the proportion it may be thought desirable to devote to armaments will be capable of wide variation by reference to the imminence and seriousness of the threat of war, the risk involved in neglecting the less probable dangers, and above all to the scale of armaments adopted by possible enemies.

The contingencies to be provided against, and the magnitude of the resources to be made available for armaments are political questions, inseparably bound up with foreign policy. When they have been decided on, the execution of the policy will be divided among:

(a) the finance department, which will raise the necessary funds;

(b) the defence departments, which will administer the funds, will raise the personnel, and procure all necessary supplies, equipment, installations and facilities;

(c) the staffs, which will plan operations appropriate to the various contingencies to be provided against;

(d) the command, which will be responsible for handling and directing the forces, and for discipline, appointments, promotions, etc.

The defence departments will depend on the command to say what they must provide, within the limits of their resources, to carry out the policy, and the command will depend on the staffs to advise what forces ought to be maintained for specified operations. Only a central governmental authority can decide what the forces are to be, by balancing the exigencies of foreign policy, on the one hand, against the proportion of the nation's resources to be devoted to the forces on the other.

The problem of defence involves many mutually dependent variables. The equations relating them cannot be worked out *a priori*; they have to be ascertained through experience. In general the solution is facilitated by the *continuity* of experience. At any one moment each variable has a definite value, and the practical question is whether its value should be altered and by how much. Even when there is a substantial change of policy or of circumstances, though the adjustments may then be greater, the pre-existing plans and establishments provide the starting point for the calculation.

The initiation of Western European Co-operation in defence is just such a change of policy for each of the partners. Each already has its own forces, and each must adapt them to the new policy. First, a common foreign policy must be agreed on to the extent that potential friends and potential enemies must be distinguished, and the nature of the warlike operations to be provided against specified. But for that purpose an authoritative representative body is required through which agreements binding on all the nations represented can be reached. As we are assuming for the present that there is not a formal federation, this representative body would be a consultative council such as has been set up under the Treaty of Brussels. We return below (pp. 108-22) to the constitutional and administrative questions involved.

The policy once agreed, it will be the responsibility of each partner to instruct its own command to co-operate in giving effect to it, and the command will then delegate staff representatives to consult with those of the other partners in preparing plans. In the first instance the plans will be confined to making the best use of the partners' existing forces. But at an early stage there will be proposals for changes calculated better to fit these forces both to co-operate with one another and to carry out the tasks anticipated. These changes will not necessarily be unfavourable to any individual countries. But there is a possibility that one of them may be called on to bear an increased burden, or the forces of another may be better adapted to the combined defence only at the cost of becoming less balanced and less effective for separate action. Such changes must evidently require the consent of the Governments which have to carry them out. Neither the staffs nor the commands can be given plenary powers at the outset to insist on plans without regard to any detrimental effects they may have on particular national interests. If military co-operation is subject from the beginning to the limiting condition that the separate identity of each country's forces and their capacity for independent action must be

47

preserved, the plans for co-ordinated operations must conform to that condition. But the application of the limiting condition to any particular plan can only be interpreted by each Government for itself. Any plan involving a division of function will to some extent make the co-operating forces mutually dependent.

Each Government will weigh the loss of independence of its forces against the additional security offered by the combined plan. The loss of independence may take two distinct forms. The forces themselves may become so specialized in certain directions as to be ill-balanced and incapable of pulling their full weight if called on to engage in operations alone. Or the production of supplies and equipment may become so specialized that the country has to procure some essentials from its allies. The adoption of plans involving specialization of either kind need not necessarily involve a reference back to the representative body responsible for policy. The participating Governments may be satisfied that the specialization does not go too far. As each Government carries out the necessary measures through its own Command, each is in a position to keep a continuing watch on anything which might impair the independence of its own armaments. In any case the representative body may be assumed to be meeting at short intervals in order to maintain co-operation in foreign policy, and will therefore offer opportunities for consultation about the revision and development of defence plans.

Specialization in the production of supplies and equipment raises somewhat different considerations from specialization in the forces themselves. Every country has to procure some part of the material required for its forces from abroad. Even if its own industry produces all the finished products required, it is sure to have to import some of the raw materials and intermediate products. In time of war it will in any case want to supplement its resources with all it can get from abroad.

Self-sufficiency is unattainable. Yet there are advantages in approaching as near to it as circumstances allow. For the Government can apply measures of requisition and direction to industrialists and workpeople within its own jurisdiction, or, even without coercive powers, can expect a response to appeals for voluntary action. If specialization is to mean that it depends on its partners for some product which it would otherwise be producing at home, it may suffer from the partners' neglect, inefficiency, or preoccupation. Especially is that to be feared if the scope of the partnership does not extend to all possible conflicts in which the country may be engaged, so that the partners responsible for the supply may be neutral. Indeed, if this is the case they may even be enemies.

It is in the event of actual war that the sources of supply become important. The preparations for war must include measures for the rapid expansion of the industries specially concerned with supplying munitions, transport, etc. There must be prior understanding with the industrialists concerned in regard to the action they will have to take. The partners, in agreeing what share each shall take in the adaptation of industry to the purposes of war, must have regard to security from attack in the location of industry, and to the productive resources available in each locality. And each partner must consider the effects of its allotted share upon its own industry; favourable effects, such as the installation of industries which will contribute to its own economic welfare; unfavourable, such as the diversion of productive resources which could be more advantageously employed otherwise, e.g. in export trade.

Each partner will also have a man-power problem. The more hands it needs in industry in wartime the fewer will it have available for the fighting forces.

DISTRIBUTION OF THE BURDEN OF DEFENCE

Distinct from the distribution of function among the partners is the distribution of burden. In the case of an alliance of the traditional limited kind, the force to be contributed by each ally has sometimes been expressly stipulated. But the usual assumption is that each ally pays for its own forces, and maintains such forces as it may think fit. The allies do not have to interfere with one another's discretion, because each can be assumed to maintain adequate armaments in its own interest. If the *casus foederis* occurs, and the alliance is involved in war, any ally that is fighting for its life may be assumed to put all its resources into the struggle. One that is not directly involved will nevertheless be at war and liable to be attacked by the enemy; it will not be expected to make a greater contribution to the common cause than its interests warrant.

D

In the case of a partnership which (a) is intended to be permanent, and (b) extends to all wars in which any of the partners may be involved, the position is different. Even though there is no merger of armaments, some safeguard is needed against any partner, in reliance on the others maintaining forces sufficient to ensure its defence, failing to make an adequate contribution.

There would certainly be very great difficulties in the way of agreeing on an apportionment of burdens. If the apportionment is approached by way of budget charges, there is no accepted criterion for determining what would be an appropriate allocation of the cost, and the problem of estimating the relative values of different money units for the purposes of such a comparison is an insoluble one.

If, on the other hand, the distribution of burdens is approached by way of an agreement on the nature and magnitude of the armaments to be maintained, the same difficulties arise as in arriving at an agreed limitation of armaments. In practice it will probably be wisest to accept the free discretion of every partner to assume whatever total burden of armaments it chooses. The mere fact that forces are to remain separate and not to be merged presupposes some interest in every partner to maintain adequate armaments.

Every partner will have entered into the association voluntarily in furtherance of its own interests; the contribution which it will undertake to make to the joint plans will correspond to the forces and supplies actually at its disposal. If at the outset the contribution seems to the other partners insufficient in relation, on the one hand, to its resources and, on the other, to its defensive needs, they can stipulate that it should arm more heavily as a condition of entering the partnership. The best safeguard against a lapse on the part of any partner from its obligation will be moral pressure. The current procedure of co-operation in defence will keep the partners fully informed of the state of one another's forces.

The question is one of *preparedness*, covering not only the peace-time establishments under arms, but the maintenance of adequate trained reserves, and of the war-potential of industry, and the dispositions for prompt mobilization both of reserves and of industry. Where the will is lacking, formal agreements and detailed definitions are unlikely to prevail on a partner to conform to the desired standards. The partnership could not afford to commit its fate to plans formed in reliance on a shirker; it would exclude the defaulting partner and withdraw support and co-operation from it. In fact the partnership must be securely founded on a continuing loyal devotion to the common cause.

It would be especially baffling at the present time to arrive at an equitable division of the burden of defence among the nations of Western Europe, seeing that they are depending on American aid even to meet the indispensable outlays on reconstruction, and can only spare anything at all for defence at the cost of severe measures of austerity. For a long time to come the internal provision of supplies and equipment for the forces of Western Europe on a peace footing, and the maintenance of an industrial war potential must be mainly in the hands of Great Britain. Obviously the British contribution itself will be very limited, and the fighting power of Western Europe will be dependent on American aid.

THE UNITED NATIONS CHARTER

The Brussels Treaty records in its preamble the purpose of the contracting parties, 'to afford assistance to each other in accordance with the Charter of the United Nations, in maintaining international peace and security and in resisting any policy of aggression'. The Treaty does not expressly claim to set up any 'regional arrangements or agency' under Article 52 of the United Nations Charter, but Article VIII of the Treaty, providing for peaceful settlement of disputes between the contracting parties themselves, would seem to create a regional arrangement conforming to the description of that Article. On the other hand Article IV, which binds the parties to afford 'all the military and other aid and assistance in their power' to any one of them who is 'the object of an armed attack in Europe', is outside the scope of Article 52, and looks for its justification to Article 51, which safeguards 'the inherent right of individual or collective self-defence if an armed attack occurs against a member of the United Nations'. 'Self-defence' is distinguished from 'enforcement' of a decision of the Security Council, the latter being provided for under Articles 42–5 of the Charter. Under Article

51

53, 'the Security Council shall, where appropriate, utilize such regional arrangement or agencies for enforcement action under its authority. But no enforcement action shall be taken under regional arrangements or by regional agencies without the authorization of the Security Council' (with the exception of measures specially reserved against ex-enemy States).

The mutual military assistance provided for by the Brussels Treaty may be described as *collective* self-defence. Article 51 apparently leaves to the judgment of the country taking action in self-defence the decision whether such armed attack as justifies the action has occurred, but the action has to be immediately reported to the Security Council, and the right to act independently in self-defence only lasts 'until the Security Council has taken the measures necessary to maintain international peace and security'. Article V of the Treaty echoes these provisions of Article 51 of the Charter. Thus the parties to the Brussels Treaty would have a free hand in defending themselves against what they regard as an armed attack, up to the stage at which the Security Council intervenes. It would then be for the Security Council to decide whether such an attack had occurred as to justify a resort to force in self-defence.

The International Organization of American States, which is to be set up under the Charter adopted at the Ninth International Conference of American States in April 1948, and which is to supersede the Treaty of Rio of 1947, is expressly stated to be a 'regional agency'. Like the Brussels Treaty, it is based on the principle of collective self-defence: 'every act of aggression by a State against the integrity or inviolability of the territory or against the sovereignty or political independence of an American State shall be considered an act of aggression against the other American States' (Article 24).

A regional agreement may mean much or little. The Brussels Treaty falls short of anything that could be called a 'union' of the parties. American opinion seems to favour something closer. The Atlantic Union now foreshadowed would no doubt in form correspond to the International Organization of American States, and in substance would provide for very close co-operation in military plans and preparations. But the United States will undoubtedly preserve complete freedom of action both in foreign policy and defence outside the commitments

U. OF ILL. LIB.

specifically necessary to combat aggression. If the Americans continue to press for closer union in Western Europe, their object will probably be that Western Europe form a unit in its relations with the United States and Canada. That should be possible without involving a formal federation.

Part II

ECONOMIC CO-OPERATION

REPORT OF THE COMMITTEE OF EUROPEAN ECONOMIC CO-OPERATION

ECONOMIC Co-operation in Western Europe became a matter of immediate practical consideration when Mr Marshall's speech of 5 June 1947 appealed for agreement among European countries on a joint programme for meeting their needs, as a condition of material support from the United States. Sixteen nations along with the military Government of Western Germany (and later Trieste) agreed to participate: Great Britain, France, Belgium, the Netherlands and Luxemburg; Norway, Sweden, Denmark, and Iceland; Austria, Italy, Greece, Turkey, Portugal, Eire, Switzerland. A Conference of Representatives of these met in Paris on 12 July 1947. A Committee of European Economic Co-operation was convened, and its Report, dated 22 September 1947, became the starting point of the plan which has since taken shape in the European Recovery Programme.

In the circumstances, the Report could be no more than a preliminary survey. 'It was impossible in a few weeks to give a completely detailed and exact account of the economic situation of sixteen European countries, of the serious difficulties confronting them, of the action which they have decided, both individually and collectively, to take, or of the import requirements necessary for the execution of such a programme.' The Report was not a 'shopping list' of the goods needed, but 'a close and careful analysis of the maladjustment which has resulted from the war, and an examination of what the participating countries can do for themselves and for each other, to work towards a lasting solution'.

The Report had to lead up to a summary of requirements, which could not be otherwise expressed than as an adverse balance of payments. In order to appreciate the problem of economic co-operation which confronts Western Europe at the present juncture, it is essential to understand the significance of this adverse balance of payments.

AN ADVERSE BALANCE CAUSED BY A CAPITAL DEFICIENCY

An independent country, if it is to remain solvent, must maintain a balance between its current external debits and credits. It must be capable of maintaining a volume of exports sufficient to pay for its imports (adjusted for the net debit or credit on current invisible items). The competitive power both of its exports and of those of its products which compete with imports depends on their cost of production in terms of foreign money units. That cost in turn depends on rates of exchange, and the condition of solvency is that a rate of exchange *can be found* consistent with the desired relation between exports and imports. Cannot the appropriate rate *always* be found, it may be asked, by the working of prices and rates of exchange in free markets? We have to show where the difficulty lies.

The economic burdens and losses of war involve a country in immediate shortages and needs, which may be so overpowering as to make fulfilment of this condition of solvency for the time being impossible. The shortages may be described as a capital deficiency. But capital here is to be taken in the widest sense; the deficiency is not merely in capital equipment, but in accumulated wealth of all kinds. Wartime destruction has to be repaired; the upkeep of plant and property has been neglected; renewals, improvements, and extensions have become overdue; traders' and consumers' stocks have been depleted.

The need to fill this capital deficiency becomes the source of an insistent demand for supplies and services, which is *additional* to the current spending out of income. It is when the stress of demand overstrains production that the unsatisfied demand attracts imports, and gives rise to a foreign exchange problem.

The special characteristic of the capital deficiency is the urgent need of *early* supplies. Disproportionate losses are sustained when production is interrupted for want of essential parts or repairs or of essential materials, or when property deteriorates for want of timely maintenance. The competitive power of an industrial concern is impaired if it cannot procure the means of making up-to-date improvements, and has to carry on with obsolete plant. Traders miss sales when their stocks are exhausted in face of an unsatisfied demand. The consumer undergoes inconvenience, discomfort, or loss of time through defect or lack in his household equipment. Gravest of all, a shortage of essentials, such as food, fuel, or shelter, may threaten to impair the working efficiency of the mass of people.

In all these instances rational calculation would justify payment of a high price for *immediate* supplies. If there were free markets, operating a free price mechanism, there would tend to be a premium offered for early delivery or early service; the premium would sift out all except those applicants who could least afford to wait, and, the needs of those having been met, prices would be so adjusted as to sift out the next batch. The premium would not necessarily fall, for the needs of the second batch might have become more pressing with the passage of time.

The sifting process depends on the deterrent effect of the premium. High prices check demand, and the premium must be a real excess of the price over some standard regarded as normal, presumably a standard corresponding to cost of production. If umbrellas which used to cost 20s. are being sold at 30s., in spite of the cost of production being unchanged, people will do without umbrellas and wait for the price to come down before they buy. But some will be so unwilling to do without them that they will pay the extra 10s. rather than wait. The 10s. which to the purchaser is a premium on early delivery, is to the seller an additional profit.

To the producers of those supplies which can only be produced at home, and therefore are not in competition with imports, the premium is an excess profit, an extra incentive stimulating production. But where the desired supplies can be procured from abroad at world prices, the exceptional demand will take effect in an excess of imports.

If the capital deficiency to be filled were moderate in amount, the excess of imports would be paid for out of monetary reserves, supplemented, if need be, by borrowing abroad. But we are now concerned with a much more serious deficiency. When reserves and foreign loans and credits are insufficient, the response of a free market to the excess of imports is a depreciation of the foreign exchange value of the money unit and world prices in terms of the unit become so much the higher. In other words the premium on early supplies is reflected in a premium on foreign exchange, and therefore in the prices of imported supplies. Thereby the high prices and excess profits are extended to those producing in competition with foreign supplies, and are in fact enjoyed by producers in general. This is an unstable position. Excess profits are sure to give rise to demands for increased wages. Employers, being eager to expand production, will be competing with one another for labour, and will readily grant the higher wages, as they can well afford to do. The rise in costs will then eat into the excess profits, and the premium on early supplies will begin to fade away.

Yet the demand for early supplies remains as insistent as ever, and is sure to restore the premium in the form of a renewed rise of prices. There will be a vicious circle of rising prices, rising wages and depreciation of the country's money in the foreign exchange market.

FREE MARKETS AND CONTROLS

That is on the assumption that there will be a sufficient supply of money (bank credit and currency) in people's hands to enable them to offer the high prices. A severe monetary policy could keep them so short of money that there would on balance be no spending in excess of incomes. The progress in filling the capital deficiency would then be limited to what is currently saved out of incomes. No doubt people directly concerned in that progress would make an exceptional effort to save on their own account. But that would not satisfy their needs, and they would endeavour to raise money from a capital market which could only offer the limited resources derived from the savings of the rest of the community.

The effect of the restrictive monetary policy would be in part to replace the premium on early supplies by a high short-term rate of interest. In fact the premium itself is simply interest in a different form. The high charge on bank advances has to act as a *deterrent* both on direct borrowing by those desiring to incur expenditure, and on borrowing by the investment market to supplement the resources it can supply to industry. (The high rate of interest might attract loans from abroad, but where a country is suffering losses and burdens which make its solvency doubtful, this is unlikely.)

Is not this a solution of the problem of an adverse balance? Why are Governments not satisfied to impose an appropriately severe monetary and fiscal policy, and to leave the rest to free markets?

The reasons are three: First, there is no certainty that the rate of progress of reconstruction would be as rapid as public policy would prescribe. Secondly, free markets would not of themselves ensure a socially equitable distribution of the supplies available for consumption. Thirdly, free markets might require excessively adverse rates of exchange, in order to preserve equilibrium in the balance of payments.

It is hardly necessary to dwell on these in detail. For the plain fact is that Governments so circumstanced do not choose to rely on free markets. Rather than depend on adverse rates of exchange to raise the prices of imported supplies and to discourage consumption, they have recourse to a direct restriction of imports.

A quantitative restriction of imports leads on to a system of controls. For the restriction of imports by itself does not necessarily reduce *consumption*; it may simply divert productive resources into supplying consumers with goods in substitution for the imports excluded. To fill the capital deficiency, a surplus of supplies over consumption is needed. In order to enlarge that surplus, the restriction of imports must be accompanied by a direct reduction of consumption, through rationing where applicable, otherwise through a limitation of supplies to the home market. Austerity thus enforced releases productive capacity and makes it available, on one side, for capital outlay and the replenishment of stocks at home, on the other, for additional exports to provide the means of procuring equivalent supplies from abroad. At the same time price control is applied to all the more widely consumed products, whether rationed or not, in order to prevent an undesirable advantage being given to the possession of money in the distribution of supplies.

If the price controls are made *fully* effective, the vicious circle of rising prices and rising wages is kept in check, and the need for a severe monetary policy to prevent inflation is obviated.

The upshot is that the balance of payments problem is the result of government intervention overriding the operation of free markets and the price mechanism. That is not to say that the whole difficulty is fictitious, and that it would not arise at all but for a misguided government interference. The impoverishment of a country may really be such that the free working of the price mechanism would give rise to intolerable anomalies and abuses. That is especially likely to occur where the impoverishment is aggravated by heavy budgetary charges for defence, and the fiscal system is overstrained.

STRONG AND WEAK COUNTRIES AND BILATERAL SETTLEMENTS

If there were only one country in this situation in a world working otherwise through free markets, its adverse balance could be treated as a single undivided net excess of imports, without regard to the relative availability of the proceeds of the country's exports to various destinations. But, when there are many countries suffering from adverse balances, that simplification becomes impossible.

The first impact of an adverse balance is on the country's monetary reserves of gold or gold equivalent. If the balance could be met without unduly depleting the reserves, there would be no problem. When the reserves are threatened with exhaustion, exchange control is resorted to to safeguard them. Exchange control maintains official rates of exchange by prohibiting dealings at any other rates, and by preventing any transactions giving rise to external indebtedness other than those expressly permitted. But, even if its efficacy in preventing a flight of capital is beyond reproach, the permitted imports may still cause an excess.

Any one country, after setting off the debits and credits arising from its transactions with each of the rest, will find a net balance remaining due to or from each. But a balance of indebtedness becoming due from another country depends for its value on the debtor country's resources and credit worthiness. Dubious debts cannot be cleared against one another, so a true multilateral settlement becomes impossible. Debts due from the economically weak countries become a matter of bilateral bargaining.

There is no hard and fast distinction between the strong and the weak. A country with a favourable balance of payments may find itself the creditor of weak countries to which it has been exporting; so far as the disposable proceeds of its current

59

transactions are concerned, it may be a debtor, and be faced by the problems of weakness. And the weakness of a weak country may in the same way be aggravated. On the other hand, a country which is classed as weak, in that on the whole it has an adverse balance, may yet be, on some part of its current transactions, a creditor of strong countries. The disposal of the foreign exchange acquired from them will be determined ultimately by its policy in regard to monetary reserves.

The very question of an adverse balance is in all cases one of monetary reserves; monetary reserves exist to pay for adverse balances, so far as these are moderate in amount and temporary in duration. When there is a capital deficiency of unmanageable amount, expedients become necessary to tide over the strain in the interval till a balance in current transactions can be restored. But during the interval prudence will permit something to be drawn from reserves, and so much the more if the reserves are being replenished by sales to strong countries.

Reserves consist essentially of exchange on strong countries. Gold ranks as a monetary reserve because it is convertible into money in the strong countries.

The strong countries are those which do not need to impose controls or import restrictions in order to safeguard their foreign exchange position. When they acquire either exchange on one another or gold, they place no obstacles in the way of its being drawn out again. Anyone in a strong country who receives foreign exchange is free, so far as his own Government is concerned, to spend it as he pleases; if occasionally disbursements abroad exceed receipts, the requisite amount will be released from reserves without question. The reserves, even though they may fluctuate, tend, on the whole, to grow.

But exchange on a weak country is not eligible for inclusion in the reserves of a strong one. Commercial banks will only hold it to the extent that they can cover themselves by forward sales. The central bank will not consent to buy it unless this is expressly provided for in a payments agreement.

A payments agreement is a part of a weak country's exchange control system. Exchange control limits the country's external payments to permitted transactions. Payments agreements apply the limitation to transactions with particular countries. Each country decides for itself what imports to procure or to allow from each, but it is only when payment comes to be made that a net balance due to one or to the other is disclosed. If the net balance has then to be paid in gold or gold equivalent, the debtor country may have to revise its import programme. A payments agreement may modify the rigour of this obligation: each party to it may undertake to accept an accumulation of money in the other up to an agreed limit, without exacting conversion into gold or strong foreign exchange. Where several countries are all suffering from grave capital deficiencies and are struggling to reconstitute their productive power, agreements of this kind introduce a desirable elasticity in allowing for inequalities of progress; those which outstrip the rest in progress towards recovery become creditors of those which fall behind; and if these latter, on regaining the lost ground, can look forward to eventually paying their indebtedness, there is here an opportunity for co-operation. Even a country suffering from a pressing capital deficiency may yet be in a position to produce surpluses of certain products, which would help in making good its neighbours' deficiencies. To sell them in markets from which nothing is to be got in return but a sterile credit would be unattractive, and, in the absence of any arrangement for co-operation, the country is likely to divert its manpower and other resources to some other use more directly related to its immediate needs, even though this involves a serious loss of productive efficiency.

MUTUAL SUPPORT OF WEAK COUNTRIES

If on the other hand several countries, all in the same state of deficiency, agree together that each will do what it can to meet the needs of the rest without regard to immediate returns, the recovery of the whole may be notably accelerated.

The controls by which austerity is imposed must in many cases divert economic resources harshly to an employment less suitable and profitable than that to which they are primarily adapted. The loss involved in the forcible conversion of resources normally employed in serving home consumption either to capital outlay at home or to export, may be a serious deduction from the gain. To reduce this loss would be a substantial advantage.

But if one distressed country is to grant credit to another, it will want to be satisfied that this other is making reasonable

61

efforts on its side to provide resources for its recovery. The former cannot be asked to pour precious supplies into an abyss of fiscal weakness, monetary collapse, and extravagant black markets. Co-operation, in fact, in the transitional period of recovery presupposes that it is really transitional, and that it will end in recovery; the measures of co-operation are inseparable from the long term measures which will come into sight when the transition is completed. The country which is allowed supplies on credit must take active steps towards its own recovery.

When recovery all round has been achieved, and monetary stability established in the group of countries, there can be mutual convertibility of money units and multilateral clearing. During the transitional period this is impossible.

If all the distressed countries have their productive resources fully employed, the advantage of any plan facilitating their mutual help will be confined to directing their productive efforts into the most fruitful or the most desirable channels. They have to provide for reconstruction, defence, and consumption, and their productive power can be applied either to meeting these needs directly or to supplying exports which will be the means of securing imports to meet them.

There may be an irreducible minimum of imports. The balance of payments problem arises from the government committing itself to a programme of imports deemed essential. But there are degrees of essentialness. For a country which cannot feed itself, imports of staple foodstuffs take the first priority. But imports of the materials necessary for the production of its exports are not far behind, since exports are the means of procuring the desired imports.

These priorities once assumed, there is still a wide range of imports which the Government may include in its programme. There will, for example, be 'incentive' products, that is to say, consumable products which people are so set on that without them they cannot be relied on to work their best. About incentive products it is difficult to generalize. Sometimes supplies of them are necessary to maintain confidence in the country's money. The workman who finds that he can only spend three or four days' wages on the things he wants, will be content to work only three or four days, unless he has a reasonable hope of being able to use the rest of a full week's pay. Saving is not attractive unless there is confidence that money is ultimately to recover its power.

Every country therefore has to maintain a tolerable supply of miscellaneous consumable goods over and above sheer necessities. These may be obtained either from at home or from abroad; if from at home, so much productive power is diverted from other uses, and may have to be replaced by imports if those uses cannot be left unsatisfied.

To the hard core of indispensable imports corresponds an indispensable minimum of exports. Apart from non-recurrent operations (drawing on monetary reserves or capital resources or grants or loans from abroad) any imports in addition to the hard core can only be obtained in exchange for additional exports. The desirability of procuring the additional imports depends upon whether that is the best use that can be made of the productive capacity employed on the additional exports. In effect it depends on a comparison of costs, that is to say, of the cost of using the productive capacity to provide the needed supplies directly, with the cost of using it to procure them indirectly through the medium of exports.

The needed supplies may be of incentive goods (or, more generally, of those which contribute to the standard of living) or they may be of goods to be used for purposes of reconstruction or of defence. *Ex hypothesi* the Government is taking responsibility for securing the supplies, because public policy will not permit their being left to the free play of markets. Price therefore will not be the governing consideration in deciding whether they are to be obtained or not. But that does not mean that *cost* should not be the governing consideration in deciding from what source they are to be obtained.

And comparison of costs cannot be altogether excluded from the weighing of the relative claims of reconstruction, defence, and the standard of living, since the question is not merely that of diverting productive resources from one of these to another, but may extend to the forcing of productive resources into an unsuitable mould. When all the productive power *readily adaptable* to reconstruction, defence, and export is being so employed, it may be that to divert some part of what remains from supplying current consumption and maintenance to any of these purposes would entail a disproportionate sacrifice.

Different criteria are appropriate to the three different purposes. Reconstruction means making up the capital deficiency. Where the productive power diverted to this purpose is less efficient than that regularly so employed, the cost is more than normal, whereas, had the productive power been used for the purposes for which it is adapted, the consumption or maintenance provided for would have been at normal cost. The excess cost disclosed is met out of the premium on early delivery.

If the productive power is not diverted to reconstruction, then the rate of progress of reconstruction is to that extent delayed. The delay means loss. If, for instance, the delay is in the renewal, improvement, or extension of capital equipment, the loss is in the postponement of the output in which the new capital equipment will bear fruit. It is against this loss that the excess cost of the diverted productive power must be weighed. A simple comparison in terms of money units may not be decisive.

Reconstruction includes not only capital outlay but the replenishment of stocks of goods. Inadequate stocks cause waste and inconvenience, queues, fruitless quests, multiplication of small purchases. The choice between reconstruction and the standard of living therefore is not a simple choice between capital equipment and consumable goods. Resources appropriate to the production of consumable goods may thus contribute to an important part of reconstruction without being diverted to any other use, provided measures of austerity keep down consumption, and so allow the accumulation of stocks.

Diversion of productive power to defence may be assumed to cause less waste through want of adaptability than diversion to capital outlay, but a considerable part of defence expenditure employs much the same kinds of productive resources as capital outlay.

The essential advantage of international trade is to avoid forcing productive power into unsuitable uses, and co-operation may relieve the strain on the productive power of the countries of Western Europe by permitting of a more appropriate international division of labour among them. The recent arrangement put forward by the Organization for European Economic Co-operation, linking the apportionment of American Aid with the supplies which the participating countries can provide for one another, aims at this advantage. It removes the obstacle which the limits imposed by payments agreements would otherwise put in the way of these supplies. There is an agreed programme of trade between the participating countries, and any country which under the programme is to be a net exporter, and fails to discharge its obligations as such, will suffer a reduction of its share of Marshall Aid dollars by the equivalent of the deficiency. In effect therefore the countries so designated will be selling for dollars.

The productive resources applied to producing these exports are diverted from other purposes. If the exports were not provided, the productive resources could be used either for reconstruction or defence, or for additional consumption, or for exports outside Western Europe which would earn an equivalent for these purposes. When the exporting country forgoes these opportunities, its need of assistance is correspondingly increased, while the needs of the participating countries to which the exports go are diminished.

It is obvious that these consequences ought to be taken into account in the apportionment of the supplies provided under the European Recovery Programme. But it is not at all clear that the apportionment is based upon the uses to which the productive resources of the several participating countries are applied. For example Great Britain relies principally on measures of austerity to maintain the export drive; producers are only allowed supplies of materials on condition that they export an assigned proportion of their output. Just because austerity is successfully enforced, and black markets kept within limits, the country's 'needs' are so much the less. On the other hand a country in which controls have broken down, and serious inroads are made by the power of money on supplies which ought to have been rationed to the mass of people, or reserved for export, can show an apparent crying need for supplies from abroad.

CO-OPERATION ARISING OUT OF THE EUROPEAN RECOVERY PROGRAMME

As military co-operation may be limited to an alliance, so economic co-operation may be limited to a temporary agreement to co-ordinate economic action for certain specified ends. The invitation in Mr Marshall's speech of 5 June did not go beyond this. He introduced it by saying: 'Europe's requirements for the next three or four years of foreign food and other essential products—principally from America—are so much greater than her present ability to pay that she must have substantial additional help, or face economic, social, and political deterioration of a very grave character.' What he asked for was agreement on a 'joint programme', and, in view of his reference to 'the next three or four years', the programme offered in the Report of the Committee of European Economic Co-operation was confined to the four years 1948–51. But whatever is done in this transitional period has a bearing upon the subsequent more permanent developments.

The two cannot be altogether dissociated. The transitional stage is to see the rehabilitation of Europe's productive power, the overtaking of the arrears of growth not merely of the war years, but of the preceding nine years, during which development was interrupted by depression and political insecurity. The task of the transitional years 1946–51 must be conceived, not as that of restoring Europe to what it was in 1929, but as that of accomplishing in six years all the progress and change appropriate to the long interval of twenty-two years.

Restoration *by itself* would mean (1) making good war damage, (2) making good arrears of maintenance and renewals of capital equipment and property, (3) replenishing stocks of goods in the hands both of traders and of consumers, (4) extensions of capital equipment, property, and stocks in proportion to the increase of population.

But rehabilitation should not mean simple reinstatement. It may be assumed that each country, in planning restoration, will take account of the innovations in equipment, methods of production, and organization which have appeared, and will instal not a mere replica but a modernized and improved equivalent of what has been destroyed or has become due for replacement. But that is not the end of the matter, for it may be desirable to redirect productive resources in various ways; the demand for a product may have expanded or contracted; new sources of supply may have been established or former sources may have dropped out; there will be opportunities for starting industries supplying entirely new products.

It is in the improvement and redirection of productive power

66

that co-operation among the countries concerned is especially needed. Much waste can be avoided by co-ordinating those developments which depart from mere reinstatement.

The programme of production recommended by the Co-operation Committee is concentrated upon food and agriculture, fuel and power, steel, timber, and transport (para. 33 of Report of 22 September 1947). For all these the maximum practicable output is likely to be the aim, and it is not in them that the need for co-operation is most conspicuous. But the modernization and extension of steel-making capacity does need to be co-ordinated, and the Committee arranged for 'the interchange of information by the steel-producing countries . . . so that each country, in developing its programme, may take account of the plans made by the others' (para. 58). And the common planning of the exploitation of new sources of electric power involves the co-operative development of resources cutting across frontiers, and the decisions are to be taken without regard to national frontiers (para. 105). Standardization of certain types of equipment (para. 108) and pooling of freight cars (para. 107) are also recommended.

More general considerations are raised with regard to trade barriers: 'the advantages which the United States has enjoyed through the existence of a large domestic market with no internal trade barriers are manifest . . . the formation of a larger free trade area in Europe could be expected to lead to greater efficiency in many sectors of production' (paras. 90–91). 'The idea of a Customs Union including as many European countries as possible is one which contains important possibilities for the economic future of Europe, and it is in the general interest that the problems involved should receive careful and detailed study by governments' (para. 92).

The French Government's declaration (para. 98) is more specific: 'that in the present state of the world only economic units sufficiently large to have at their disposal an important home market are able to lower the price of industrial and agricultural production sufficiently to ensure, thanks to better technique, an improved standard of living for their people, and to allow the countries concerned to withstand world-wide competition; that the present division of Europe into small economic units does not correspond to the needs of modern competition;

and that it will be possible with the help of Customs Unions to construct larger units on the strictly economic plane.' The implication is that Western Europe with its 270 million inhabitants ought to be able to rival American achievements in mass production, provided it can start with sufficient protection of its united markets.

The economic life of the world has become lopsided. The predominance of the United States has been attributable in the first instance to unrivalled natural resources, not only an acreage of cultivable land far exceeding what is necessary to supply the whole population, but abundant mineral resources, including, besides metallic ores and oil, coal seams of exceptional productivity. But the present century has added to these advantages the development by American initiative of mass production. The proposal of the Co-operation Committee, to improve the relative position of Western Europe by creating the conditions in which mass production can prosper, raises several difficult questions, and we return to the subject below.

DISCREPANT STANDARDS OF AUSTERITY

In the nineteenth century, when war could be regarded as an aberration from normal economic life, and the gold standard (along with bimetallism) supplied an international currency, the principal impediment placed by national frontiers in the way of economic intercourse took the shape of protective import duties. Between 1815 and 1914 there was no world war: the wars which actually occurred were localized, and with few exceptions were short; the total mobilization of economic life was not thought of. The case made by Cobden and his contemporaries for free trade was not merely that the complete suppression of protective tariffs by all countries would bear fruit in a more perfect geographical division of labour, but that the removal of the only remaining concrete embodiment of economic exclusiveness would weld the whole world into a unity of interdependent communities, and make for universal peace.

The twentieth century seems to have rendered peace no better than an interval between wars; at any rate the economic jurisdiction of the sovereign State, of which national frontiers mark the boundaries, has to be regarded as an instrument of warfare no less than of welfare. And, even from the economic standpoint, direct restrictions on imports and on exchange transactions have thrown import duties into the shade. A customs union or a free-trade area as defined by the Havana Charter (Article 44[4]) implies the suppression within it not only of duties but of 'other restrictive regulations of commerce'. In considering the problems of Western European Union in the circumstances of the present day, the question of suppressing import restrictions takes precedence over any matters of import duties.

What prospect is there of suppressing import restrictions and exchange restrictions within a Western European Union? We have seen that the restrictions may be due to either or both of two distinct conditions: a capital deficiency, or a monetary weakness. Where both are present, both must be remedied before the restrictions can be dispensed with.

Import restrictions, in themselves, have the same protective effect as import duties: the exclusion or limitation of foreign competition stimulates home industries. But, when import restrictions are resorted to in consequence of a capital deficiency, they are part of a design to enforce a reduction of consumption; to divert productive resources at home into supplying goods in place of those excluded would be inconsistent with that object. Accordingly, as we have seen, the restriction of imports is associated with a limitation of home-produced supplies to the home market, and the effect is austerity.

This limitation of the disposal of home-produced supplies is only helpful in so far as the supplies withheld or the productive power released can be otherwise employed without undue loss of value. So much discrimination against foreign supplies as may be required to secure a market for such part of the home supplies as does not fulfil this condition will be justifiable. But when countries of Western Europe impose restrictions upon imports from one another, and apply against them the discrimination appropriate to foreign supplies, they may be retarding one another's recovery.

Nor is that the only consideration involved. One of the most important of invisible imports is travellers' expenditure. Restriction upon their expenditure really means an interference with personal contacts between individuals of different countries. Are not all steps towards closer union liable to be frustrated so long as the ordinary people of Western Europe are disunited and separated as never before?

If all were applying the same degree of austerity (and if economic conditions were in other respects sufficiently nearly homogeneous), their restrictions against one another might be wholly abandoned, and the production and disposal of restricted commodities dealt with for their combined territories as a single unit. But the degree of austerity imposed varies widely from one country of Western Europe to another. Great Britain in particular is suffering heavily from the loss of external assets and from the burden of a new external indebtedness in addition to the destruction and depletion of resources at home. Moreover Great Britain alone has made a success of the enforcement of controls.

It would be quite impossible to enforce the British system of controls in all its rigour on Western Europe, nor could Great Britain afford to relax the controls on which her solvency depends. This may well be a long-period question, to be considered in connexion with that of discrepant standards of living. Meanwhile the question of controls and restrictions on trade in the short period is intimately connected with that of monetary policy. Import restrictions are imposed to guard against the adverse balance which a lapse into inflation threatens to induce. A deficiency of real resources may take a long time to remedy. A weak or lax monetary policy calls for prompt corrective measures. Import restrictions and exchange controls are no more than palliatives, and no real progress can be made in economic rehabilitation till the monetary disorders are surmounted by means of a radical remedy.

INFLATION AND MONETARY REFORMS

The first requisite is likely to be the restoration of a sound budgetary position; so long as budget deficits are being met by the creation of credit, the country's money will not command confidence. This is a matter in which each country must rely on its own efforts. That does not mean that its task may not be facilitated by help from abroad. Austria obtained an invaluable breathing space in surmounting her fiscal difficulties from the League of Nations Loan of 1922. And in Western Europe the receipt by governments of the proceeds of sale of supplies provided under the European Recovery Programme will be a budgetary resource, in so far as the proceeds have to be applied to redeem indebtedness. For when there is a deficit, new indebtedness is being incurred, and this resource will mean so much the less inflationary borrowing from the banks.

The present monetary conditions of the countries of Western Europe exhibit wide differences. If Greece be left out of account, those of the participants in the European Recovery Programme which have suffered severely from inflation are France, Italy and Western Germany. Since the appearance of the Sixteen Nations' Report in September 1947, Italy has made notable and successful efforts to gain control of her monetary situation; a substantial fall has been brought about in the price level, and the foreign exchange value of the lira has been held firm, but it is too soon to assume that a permanent recovery has yet been assured. France on the other hand is still in a very precarious situation. A heavy budget deficit continues to undermine confidence in the money, and it is found impossible to check the rising tide of prices and wages by means of controls. The resulting labour unrest opens the way to communist influence and has disastrous political reactions. The budget of 1949 represents one more effort to restore financial order, but it is not possible to say whether it is destined to succeed. Needless to say this state of monetary instability is an obstacle in the way of recovery. There is not only a direct loss of output through strikes, but the pressure of inflationary demand makes the enforcement of controls impossible, and the procurement of adequate supplies for the rationing system is obstructed by the prevailing distrust of the money.

Western Germany was entangled in even more serious monetary troubles up to June 1948, when a thorough monetary reform was put into effect. Controls on both wages and prices had been successfully enforced by the Nazis since 1936, and had continued to be enforced under the military Governments. But the disparity between the controlled prices and wages and the quantity of money in circulation was so great that confidence in the money was completely lost, and, apart from the spending of controlled wages on rationed supplies, business was carried on almost exclusively by barter. The monetary reform eliminated the redundant money and restored confidence, and remarkable progress has since been achieved towards the restoration of normal economic life. Western Germany it may be mentioned had the advantage of the financial and economic backing of the occupying Powers. The United States and Great Britain took the responsibility of meeting the absolutely essential needs of the population, and their help incidentally furnished a solution of the budget troubles. The help now forthcoming under the European Recovery Programme ought greatly to facilitate the solution of the monetary troubles of France.

In other nations of Western Europe inflation is not so acute. In the United Kingdom the same controls which have enforced austerity have fended off inflation; they have prevented the excessive supply of money from taking effect in excessive spending. Spending on consumption has been restricted by the limitation of supplies to the home market, combined with the control of prices; capital outlay has been restricted by control of capital issues, by licensing, by allocation of scarce materials, and by exchange control. Thus the controls have prevented the vicious circle of rising prices and rising wages from being joined. If their success has not been complete, that is partly because the link of the British to the American monetary system through the fixed rate of exchange between the pound and the dollar has infected the pound with the inflationary tendency to which the dollar has been subject since the removal of the American price controls in 1946.

Some of the countries of Western Europe have applied a more thorough treatment; instead of preventing the redundant money from being spent, they have extinguished it by means of forced loans. In this procedure Belgium led the way in October 1944, and achieved a notable success in spite of subsequent difficulties. As the Belgian Government claimed in its declaration to the Committee of European Economic Co-operation (Volume II, p. 312), 'Belgium's monetary experiment is by way of becoming classic'. Holland, Norway, and Austria have followed the Belgian example with favourable results. (Austria, like Western Germany, extinguished a part of the currency without giving holders any equivalent).

Of the remaining monetary systems of Western Europe, those of Switzerland and Portugal came through the war actually strengthened and those of Sweden and Denmark not seriously weakened.

On the whole there may be said to be a reasonable prospect of the restoration of monetary order. Nevertheless there is a contingency which may threaten a recrudescence of the trouble. The progress of inflation in the United States has for some time been a cause of anxiety, and it is probable that the American administration and Congress will sooner or later take strong measures to stop it. It is only too likely that the result will be a deflation such as that of the years 1920–2, which caused acute embarrassment to all those countries which were taking the dollar value of their money units as the criterion of monetary soundness. For two or three years countries which have linked their money units to the dollar (and therefore to gold) have been in the position of a fleet of sailing vessels keeping company with a leader which is continually losing way to leeward; when the leader eventually starts making good the loss by beating to windward, the followers will be confronted with the choice of facing the same struggle or parting company.

A CUSTOMS UNION

In discussions of closer economic union of Western Europe the project of a customs union nearly always comes under consideration. A protective tariff discriminates in favour of home producers, and therefore against foreign producers. If then the countries of Western Europe retain their separate tariffs, they will be discriminating against one another. The very reverse of co-operation.

If on the contrary, by forming a customs union, they suppress all protective duties against imports from one another, they will not only be ceasing to discriminate against one another, but will be discriminating in favour of one another. Thus would a start be made in co-operation of a positive kind.

Whereas monetary reform and the removal of quantitative restrictions on trade are transitional problems affecting co-operation in the short period, a customs union is a long-period affair. Nevertheless even a proposal for a customs union has to be approached from the point of view of its short-period effects. Any long-term policy, however desirable its ulterior effects, can only be justified subject to the condition that it does not retard or impede the vital progress of recovery and reconstruction.

The recommendations in favour of a customs union, quoted above (p. 67-8) from the Report of the Committee of European Economic Co-operation, were prompted from America. Sir Oliver Franks, in introducing the subject to the Committee, said: 'We have gathered from Mr Clayton that the creation of preferential tariff groups would not commend itself to American opinion without a definite undertaking to form an eventual customs union.'

The distinction is paradoxical. If we suppress duties on goods imported from our friends altogether, we are making a bigger discrimination against the rest of the world than if we merely exact duties at reduced preferential rates. Why does American policy accept the greater discrimination and reject the less?

The most substantial reason perhaps is that a customs union, once established, is a permanency: the tariff policy of the customs union may change from time to time, but the commercial relations of the partners with one another are fixed once and for all on a footing of mutual free trade. On the other hand preferential tariffs, being a matter of a little more or a little less, are susceptible of perpetual variation, and every change is likely to have repercussions on the relations, both commercial and political, between each of the parties and outside nations. Any change in the protective effect of a tariff inflicts a *discontinuity* of conditions on all the exporting interests concerned. A new preference given to one is especially injurious to the rest when all are under-employed, and it was the prevalence of vexatious changes in trade barriers during the depression of the nineteen-thirties that provoked American antagonism to any form of discrimination in international trade, other than a straight import tariff.

On the political side preferences in favour of some countries discriminate against others: in proportion as they show a friendly disposition to the former, they show an unfriendly disposition to the latter. They are therefore liable to be a prolific source of international friction. Against that danger a safeguard was found in the nineteenth century in a general adoption of the most-favoured-nation clause, active support of which is a feature of the American trade policy. The preferential tariffs agreed on by the Commonwealth at Ottawa in 1932 have always been resented by the Americans as discriminating against their products. A customs union on the other hand creates so close a bond between the participating countries, that, even if it does not lead up to formal federation, the discriminatory effect against the rest of the world is a relatively insignificant factor. And in any case Americans would be on insecure ground in discountenancing a policy of which the customs union of their own forty-eight States is constantly commended as the best working model.

In the Report of the Committee of European Economic Co-operation that example was quoted, and a customs union was recommended as an object of study, to the exclusion of tariff preferences (p. 67 above).

A customs union pools the policy of the participating countries in respect of protective tariffs. The essence of that branch of policy is that an import duty on any product makes possible a difference between the price of the product at home and the price abroad. If there is no equivalent excise duty on the home-produced article, the home producer is favoured either by making a bigger profit or by being enabled to maintain his sales in spite of higher costs.

Quantitative restrictions of imports can be used to maintain a wider price difference than any import duties which fall short of being prohibitive. But they are not necessarily used for that purpose. And where the aim is not the protection of home producers but the restriction of consumption, the effect of the price difference on producers may be wholly or partly counter-acted by an excise duty, such as the purchase tax. In fact it is a mistake to suppose that quantitative restrictions supersede the protective policy of an import tariff. The appropriate price differences are kept in view, and controls are likely to be so applied as to prevent goods being either produced at costs or sold at prices above or below those consistent with the accepted protective policy. That is to say, controlled prices will allow no more than a reasonable margin above costs, and production at excessive cost will be discouraged.

If the strains of the transitional period in Western Europe are presently to be eased, and controls and quantitative restrictions to be dispensed with, the structure of tariff protection which will emerge will not necessarily be fundamentally changed. And any change in the preferential margin of price secured to the home producer, even while the quantitative restrictions are still in force, will work its due effect in encouraging production or the reverse.

Therefore the effects of a customs union brought into operation during the transitional period are to be looked for in these price margins. Entry into a customs union modifies the price margins. To producers in one of the member countries who are able to supply consumers or users in another with an article which is subject to a protective import duty, the price margin gives an advantage not only over producers outside the union but over those producers in the importing country who have adapted their business to the protected price.

Increased supplies from the other countries inside the customs union will tend to displace imports from outside it, and also supplies previously produced within the importing country. Under conditions of full employment these increased supplies can only be provided by diverting to the producers productive resources (labour at any rate, and probably also new plant) which would have been available for other purposes. What is involved is a transfer of productive resources from one set of industries to another. The new distribution of productive power may or may not be an improvement in the long run, but the transfer in itself is certain to cause loss.

Controls however (which in the transitional period may be assumed still to be operative) can be so applied as to prevent consequences which are thought to be undesirable. Import restrictions in the importing country can keep its total imports of the product unchanged, so that there would be no displacement of its own producers. Any increase in imports from within the customs union would then be balanced by a decrease in imports from outside.

Thus controls can be used to postpone the dislocation which free trade within the customs union would otherwise cause to industries previously protected from competitors within the union, and a gradual withdrawal of the controls spread over a period of years might ease the adjustment of these industries to the loss of protection when the controls are finally abandoned.

The immediate effect on exporters from outside the union remains. Their loss of business corresponds to the gain made by the exporters within it; yet it is not to be taken for granted that no dislocation is involved in the countries where these latter work.

There may be no change in their output of the products in

question; that is to say, their exports to markets within the union may simply take the place of equal exports to markets outside it. For the customs union as a whole imports and exports are then equally reduced. But it is more likely that there will be some increase in output, and the diminution in imports will not be offset, at any rate will not be wholly offset, by a diminution in exports.

As already pointed out (above, pp. 61-4), if full employment be assumed, the increase in output can only be at the expense of a decrease in some other direction. The decrease may be in exports of other products, or in supplies for home consumption, or in capital outlay and reconstruction. The loss of resources under the latter heads may be wholly or partly made up by increased imports.

These developments will be felt even when controls remain in operation, and will take full effect when controls are abandoned. How far they are conducive to the economic interests of the countries constituting the customs union depends on factors which will be very difficult to ascertain or to assess. They in any case affect adversely those producers outside the union who lose markets within it.

A customs union of Western Europe would exclude the Dominions. They have never been willing to agree to a customs union of the Commonwealth itself, for they have felt the necessity of protecting their own manufacturers against the competition of long-established British industries; only so could they save themselves from the fate for which Cobden destined them, 'to be hewers of wood and drawers of water' for the United Kingdom.

Yet a position in which all imports from Western Europe into the United Kingdom were duty free, and imports from the Commonwealth paid duty (even though at lower rates than from the rest of the world) could hardly be defended. There would be products imported from Western Europe with which no Commonwealth producers would wish to compete, and which could be nominally admitted free of duty from the Commonwealth as well as from Western Europe. But there would certainly be some in which producers in Great Britain, in the Dominions, and in Western Europe would be in active competition. Butter is an obvious example. The British producer wants to be protected against the Dominion producer, and the Dominion producer wants a preference against the European producer. Their claims could only be reconciled with free imports of the European product by a recourse to subsidies, either direct or disguised under Government bulk buying. A fiscal morass! And in any case to employ subsidies in place of duties to discriminate against the other members of the customs union would be a direct contravention of the principles of the union.

A CUSTOMS UNION AS A PRELUDE TO FORMAL FEDERATION

On the occasion when the question of a customs union came before the Committee on European Economic Co-operation (above, p. 74), Sir Oliver Franks said: 'The importance of the idea of customs unions resides primarily in the fact that, if their eventual formation could be undertaken now, it would point the way to a new degree of stability and interdependence of a European economy in the future.'

Whatever the balance of economic advantage may be, a customs union does undoubtedly conduce to the mutual dependence of the countries forming it. Each depends on the others, both for markets for some of its industries, and for the supply of some of the products which it needs to import. The customs union imposes upon them a common commercial policy in their international relations, and a merger of their revenues from indirect taxes—a merger not only of customs, but of excise duties, for a difference in excise duties on any commodity involves a price difference, to balance which there must be an equivalent import duty, and consequently a customs barrier at which the duty can be levied.

There must be a single joint authority responsible for tariff policy and for indirect taxes; it must be constituted by the participating countries, and either be representative of them or receive from them a delegated power of making decisions binding on the entire customs union.

In fiscal policy it is hardly possible to separate the sphere of indirect taxes from that of public finance as a whole. Fiscal policy is concerned with Government expenditure as a whole and the apportionment of the consequent burden of taxation among the possible heads of revenue, and among classes and categories of taxpayers. The apportionment between indirect taxes and the rest (or even between customs revenues alone and the rest) is itself an important part of the policy as a whole.

A customs union requires the indirect taxes to be pooled in the hands of the joint authority. If each member State retains the responsibility for the whole of its government expenditure, the proceeds of the indirect taxes must be apportioned—each country presumably getting what its own consumers have contributed. The apportionment can be estimated, or, if the data are not sufficient to support agreed estimates, a system of customs barriers can be maintained for statistical purposes.

The finance ministers of the member countries will find one part of their revenue determined outside their control; they will no doubt be in a position to influence the decisions of the joint authority which determines the customs tariff, but in the end must submit to them. The joint authority itself will endeavour, so far as tariff policy allows, to adapt its fiscal policy to the aims of the finance ministers, but it can best avoid confusion and conflicting aims by leading rather than following; fiscal policy for the whole customs union is likely to fall largely into its hands. And it is hardly necessary to say that a fiscal union is an important, even a decisive, instalment of a formal federation.

Moreover the common tariff policy itself points very definitely in the same direction. Every commercial treaty affects the relations of the countries negotiating it—often with third countries as well as with one another—and the foreign ministers of the countries forming the customs union, no less than the finance ministers, must accommodate themselves to the proceedings of the joint authority.

A common tariff policy is also closely bound up with industrial policy. A protective tariff is only maintained at all because it is believed to have beneficial effects on the economic life of the community, whether by promoting a diversification of activity, or by establishing infant industries, or by preserving existing industries from the distress and loss caused by new or intensified foreign competition. And evidently these objects cannot be isolated from general economic policy.

We may conclude that a customs union would almost certainly be found to be the prelude to a formal federation. The German Zollverein is a significant precedent. And probably most of the advocates of a customs union would see it in this light. A customs union is not usually recommended in isolation, but as supplementary to a closer political and military co-operation. The case for a customs union may be said to stand or fall with the case for formal federation. That case we examine below (pp. 101-8).

MODIFIED CUSTOMS UNION PROPOSALS

It is with a view to opening the way to the removal of mutual tariff barriers by an association less close than a customs union that provision has been made in the Havana Charter of the International Trade Organization for what is called a 'free-trade area'. By that is understood a group of countries which suppress barriers on imports from one another, but retain their freedom to impose different rates of duty on imports from outside countries. There need then be no joint tariff authority, no pooling of revenues, and no commitment to formal federation.

But it is open to serious doubt whether this compromise is practicable. In general an import duty (if operative) causes an equivalent price difference; the price of the dutiable commodity being raised above the price in world markets by the amount of the duty. Consequently a difference between rates of import duty in two countries corresponds to a price difference between them. The existence of such difference between the prices of the same commodity on opposite sides of a frontier can only be maintained if a duty balancing the difference is charged at the frontier. If such duties are charged, the system becomes one not of a free trade area at all, but of tariff preferences such as neither the Charter nor the most-favoured-nation clause would allow.

Every member country whose rate of duty on a product imported from outside the union is higher than the lowest so charged by any member, would charge on imports of the product from other members a countervailing duty equal to the difference between its own rate of duty and the lowest. In fact the preference accorded by the member countries to one another on any product would be an abatement of duty equal to the lowest rate charged by any member on imports of that product from outside.

Thus if there are five members and they charge respectively 10, 10, 15, 20, and 25 per cent *ad valorem* on imports of shoes from outside the union, the two charging 10 per cent will admit shoes from one another and from the other three free of duty, while the other three will charge 5, 10, and 15 per cent respectively on all shoes procured from any of the members. (A relatively high duty is probably inoperative if the member country charging it is an exporter of shoes.)

The formation in Western Europe of a free trade area of the kind defined by the I.T.O. Charter has been advocated on the ground that the United Kingdom could enter it without giving up the Commonwealth tariff preferences. But if there were no system of countervailing duties, Commonwealth producers would still have to face the competition of free imports from Western Europe. And, if there were countervailing duties, the United Kingdom could only give a preference to them on a product on which the British rate of duty was higher than the lowest charged by any member of the union.

It would evidently be a mistake to count on the establishment of a customs union of Western Europe including the United Kingdom, even at any future time. And, that being so, the existing tendency to form partial customs unions is one to be viewed with serious misgivings. Of these partial customs unions, only one, the Benelux union, comprising Belgium, the Netherlands, and Luxembourg, is actually in operation, and even there in some respects only provisional arrangements have been possible. A project for a Franco-Italian customs union has been favourably reported on, and is under consideration between the two Governments. Proposals for economic co-operation between Norway, Sweden, Denmark, and Iceland, are in an inchoate stage and do not as yet definitely include a customs union in their objectives.

Each of the customs unions contemplated would have the effect of discriminating against the supply by any country outside to one of the members of goods which another member can supply. It is a mistake to suppose that the establishment of these partial customs unions would be a step towards a single Western European customs union. A customs union once formed is not easily extended. Vested interests will have been created in the protective effect of the union itself. The existing participants and a new entrant will alike find some of their industries exposed to a new competition, and the advantage to some industries of enjoying a newly protected market will not outweigh the dislocation caused. If for example Western Europe formed a customs union, and all the industries of the participating countries were adjusted to that state of things, it would be difficult for Czechoslovakia or Hungary to enter the union after opportunities which the union might have offered them at the outset have already been filled by producers within the original union.

Therefore it is not wise to suppose that the membership of a customs union can be built up by stages; all the countries ultimately to be included in it should be committed at the outset. The actual removals and adjustments of duties may reasonably be spread over a period of years in order to minimize the dislocating effects, but the ultimate form of the union as well as its membership should be determined from the start.

If partial customs unions, such as Benelux and the Franco-Italian, are formed in the near future, they may be found later on to have irretrievably prejudiced both their junction together, and the adhesion of other countries of Western Europe, and in particular of the United Kingdom. Worst of all from the British point of view, the obstacles to an amalgamation of the separate customs unions might be overcome, and a single Western European customs union formed excluding the United Kingdom. Every British exporter to a country of Western Europe would then have to pay duties from which all his competitors within the customs union would be exempt. Resistance from those competitors might become an insurmountable bar to the admission of the United Kingdom to the customs union. Over and above the adverse effect upon the British balance of payments and standard of living (an effect which, after the first dislocation, could probably be fairly well lived down), this development would obviously expose the whole cause of Western European co-operation to a threat of weakening, if not of disruption.

It was, no doubt, a consciousness of the difficulties in the way of a Western European customs union that led those who took part in the Havana Conference to make exceptions to the general rule of no discrimination in favour of less complete forms of preference. One of these, the free trade area, has been shown above (p. 80-1) not to be a very hopeful departure. Another is contained in Article 15 of the Charter.

We referred above (p. 67) to the declaration made by the French Government to the Committee on European Economic

Co-operation in favour of a customs union (paragraph 98 of Committee's Report). The aim of that declaration was to provide a market co-extensive with Western Europe for mass-producing industries. The fostering of 'infant industries' has long been accepted as a legitimate ground for a policy of protective tariffs, and a mass-producing industry is an especially suitable subject for that treatment. Mass-production means a combination of plant and organization adapted to a very large output and capable of producing at very low cost, provided it is fully employed. Once a market big enough to take its full output is assured, it can compete on equal terms with other mass-producers, and can easily outbid smaller concerns.

If mass-producing industries could be established in Western Europe, its dependence on the United States for their products might be brought to an end, or at any rate diminished.

To provide a sheltered market for European mass-producing industries, a full customs union is not necessary. An arrangement limited to the products of those industries would suffice. Article 15 of the Havana Charter contemplates 'preferential agreements' for economic development and reconstruction. It allows countries belonging to the same 'economic region' to grant one another preference or freedom from duties, 'to ensure a sound and adequate market for a particular industry'.

The countries of Western Europe, for instance, might promote the mass production of motor vehicles by eliminating all import duties on those produced by one another, and maintaining duties on those produced elsewhere. They would reserve their own market of some 200 million people for the favoured industries, while keeping their tariff policies in all other respects unaffected and independent. This arrangement, however, would be permitted only for a limited period, ten years, with a possible extension to fifteen, subject to the approval of the International Trade Organization. The assumption is that by that time either the infant industries will have grown up, or the experiment will not deserve to be continued.

To take advantage of Article 15, there must be co-operation not only between the Governments but between the industrialists concerned. The products to be favoured must be agreed on, and, once they have been selected, the development of the industries can hardly be left to wait upon the hazards of private enterprise.

Protection in the United States and Germany bore fruit in a great industrial development, but the infant industries took a generation or two to reach maturity. Governments will not agree on a preferential arrangement to protect an industry unless they can ensure prompt action by the industry to take advantage of it. That is a matter of planning to which we return below (pp. 87-95).

A preferential agreement under Article 15 would discriminate against producers outside it, in the same way as a full customs union. A preference calculated to favour mass-producing industries in Western Europe would discriminate more particularly against the United States, the home of mass-production.

Would that provoke opposition from the United States? Not necessarily. For the mass-producing industries include some of those most essential to a country's war potential. If Western Europe is well equipped in this respect, the demands it must make on the United States, in the event of their being allies in war, or in preparation for that contingency, will be so much the less. American mass-producing industries do not seriously need external markets, especially at the present time, when they are still overtaking their home demand, and the European demand for any American products is seen to be dependent on a general revival of European economic life.

MONETARY CO-OPERATION

That monetary inflation is a serious, perhaps insurmountable, obstacle to economic co-operation is well recognized. The countries participating in the European Recovery Programme have undertaken to take the necessary measures to stop it or to prevent it. But to say that economic co-operation presupposes the establishment of monetary order in the co-operating countries is an understatement. No country, whether co-operating with others or not, can afford to subject itself to an indefinite continuance of monetary disorder. Disorder here means in most cases extravagant inflation, though deflation, such as prevailed in the nineteen-thirties, is no less devastating.

Therefore, in looking beyond the near future, it is legitimate to assume that the countries of Western Europe will have regained control of their monetary affairs. That means that each will be in a position to prevent undue fluctuations in the *internal* value or purchasing power of its money unit. The Central Bank of issue or other agency providing the community with currency may be assumed to be able to regulate the flow of money, provided its operations are not frustrated by renewed disturbances originating on the side of government finance.

Stabilization of the internal values of the money units of the co-operating countries ought to bring with it a near approach to stabilization of their external values, at any rate, of their rates of exchange in terms of one another. The acute troubles of the foreign exchanges, from which the world has suffered since 1918, have been due to instability of the *internal* values of money units. More particularly when a unit, such as the pound or the dollar, which is taken by a number of countries as the fixed basis of parity, itself becomes seriously unstable, the monetary systems of these other countries are infected with the disorder. We have referred above (p. 73) to the disastrous effect of the American deflation of 1920–22 upon countries which were trying to regain parity with the dollar, and to the danger that the inflation which has for some time been in progress in the United States may have a sequel like that of 1919–20. The American deflation of 1930–33 is an even more ominous instance. These are cases where the dollar has remained linked to gold, and has carried gold with it, so that the foundation offered to money by gold itself has been no less treacherous.

Regulation of the internal value of a country's money unit, while directly governed by credit policy, cannot be dissociated from the unit's external value, that is to say, from rates of exchange. A fixed gold parity means a fixed parity in terms of other money units similarly fixed. When the gold standard is in abeyance, monetary authorities still look to rates of exchange for guidance; the most direct symptoms of an undue monetary expansion or contraction are usually in the balance of payments and in rates of exchange.

But rates of exchange only measure the *relative* values of money units; fixing them does not prevent a concomitant inflation or deflation throughout the whole group of related units. Countries relying entirely on keeping rates of exchange on one another unvarying are like the blind leading the blind. They need a leader, a monetary authority with an *independent* policy.

Monetary co-operation in fact takes the form of following a

leader. At the present time the leader is the United States. The traditional leadership of London has not been entirely superseded; not only does the Sterling Area form a group of money units linked directly to the pound sterling, but there are countries outside the Sterling Area whose holdings of sterling form an important part of their monetary reserves.

But as things are the pound sterling itself accepts the leadership of the American dollar. The hard core of imports which the British Government deems necessary, and either procures or permits, causes an adverse balance which, even with American aid, can only be kept within practicable limits by means of far-reaching controls. Whether wisely or not, the severe policy of austerity has not been accompanied by a severe monetary policy (p. 57 above), and the pressure of potential inflation is continually felt. The monetary reserves have barely been saved from exhaustion by a rigorous exchange control, which keeps down the resources of foreign exchange that may be privately held to an indispensable minimum, restricts external investment, and limits the uses to which foreign-held sterling may be put.

Economic weakness in these various forms does undoubtedly put Great Britain at a disadvantage in seeking to regain her position of monetary leadership. Nevertheless, within the limits of Western Europe, her claims to exercise such leadership are already clear. Not only does she provide the channel through which supplies come from the Sterling Area, but she heads the list of countries which are supplying their neighbours with necessary imports within the scope of the European Recovery Programme.

In a wider view, London's past position as a monetary centre and a credit centre has been a by-product of British mercantile enterprise. British mercantile experience and skill remain in existence, and the world needs the services they can render as much as ever. Monetary co-operation in Western Europe is therefore likely to mean co-operation with Great Britain. At the same time there will be the same need of monetary stability in the rest of the world, and whatever Western Europe does in this direction will tend to be merged in a worldwide scheme.

The International Monetary Fund has been devised to maintain fixed rates of exchange, only to be disturbed in any particular case on the ground of a 'fundamental disequilibrium'. One of the purposes of the Fund is 'to assist in the establishment of a multilateral system of payments in respect of current transactions between members, and in the elimination of foreign exchange restrictions which hamper the growth of world trade'.

Fixed rates of exchange do not of themselves assure multilateral settlements. To secure confidence, they must correspond to comparative costs, and must be free from disturbance on either side, either by an adverse balance arising from a capital deficiency, or by the pressure of active or suppressed inflation. Only when these conditions are fulfilled will the Governments concerned be in effective command of their monetary affairs. Even so, if multilateral settlements and mutual convertibility of money units are to be securely founded, the regulative power acquired, especially by the monetary authorities responsible for the leading currencies, must be so exercised as to maintain stability of purchasing power in the whole system of money units.

Unvarying rates of exchange firmly founded on stable internal values of the money units offer all the substantial advantages to be obtained from monetary co-operation. A monetary *union* of Western Europe, meaning the use of a common currency, would be important rather for its political implications than for its economic. It would involve the surrender by the participating governments of their freedom to issue their own separate fiduciary currencies. Bank credit and other indebtedness throughout the union would be legally payable in a hand-to-hand currency common to all the participating countries. There must be a single note-issuing authority for all; in effect a single Central Bank for the union.

The credit system is dependent on the currency system, for the cash reserves of the banks depend in the last resort on the note-issuing authority's operations in issuing and withdrawing currency. The expansions and contractions of the flow of money, upon which full employment and unemployment depend, are in the hands of the note-issuing authority. Even if the Central Bank's old-time independence of fiscal policy is preserved, the unification of monetary policy is a very long step towards a unification of economic policy. The modern fashion of linking employment policy to budget policy, would necessitate something like a unification of fiscal policy. And in any case the Central

Bank's independence of fiscal policy is a fair weather principle. In case of war or other emergency a Government may find itself unable to procure the funds to meet urgent payments by any other means than bank advances, and no Government can afford to cut itself off from that expedient. If the currency is in the hands of an authority outside its control, the Government may find bank advances beyond a limit denied to it; it is then at a crucial moment that the monetary authority (and therefore the monetary union as a whole to which that authority is subordinate) holds the purse strings.

Bank advances beyond the prudent limit are inflationary—therefore, it may be said, illegitimate. And no doubt a monetary union might exert a salutary influence by preventing a government transgressing the limit. But there are occasions when the means of payment must be provided if defeat or other commensurate disaster is to be avoided. And even in quiet times government finance involves large floating debt transactions in which the co-operation of the Central Bank cannot be dispensed with. And its co-operation means a share in the policy upon which the indebtedness depends.

A common currency would almost certainly mean fiscal union, and fiscal union means formal federation.

Have there not been monetary unions in the past, it may be asked, which had no such effect? The Latin Union of 1865 bound France, Italy, Belgium, and Switzerland to employ a common system of standard coins, those minted by each country being legal tender in the other three. But the Latin Union did not limit the freedom of the participating countries in the vital matter of the issue of fiduciary currency. And as it turned out, both France and Italy issued inconvertible paper currencies during the continuance of the Union.

JOINT PLANNING

A customs union or a monetary union marks out a field for international co-operation. But neither, once established, necessarily involves continuing co-operation. Either kind of union brings into being an *institution* to which national action has to conform, and once the union is there, the action of each nation may be taken in entire independence of that of the rest.

Beyond such established institutions there is a wide field for economic co-operation. When we speak of economic co-operation, we have primarily in mind (though not perhaps exclusively) the co-operation of *Governments*. Governments are the guardians and interpreters of public policy, and co-operation among nations means directing public policy to a common purpose. Economic planning, a much overworked phrase, means bringing economic activity by government guidance into conformity with the aims of public policy. Planning has reference to a future period, long or short; so economic planning does not include regimentation and controls adopted to meet immediate exigencies. On the other hand it does include the longer term considerations which are taken into account in shaping these measures.

An import tariff, with its offshoots in the form of a customs union or a system of commercial treaties, is not itself a plan. The planning is done by those who frame the tariff or negotiate the treaties. They hope to see certain effects on the country's economic life; but, if the realization of those effects is left to private enterprise, the planning does no more than provide the setting for the desired developments; the planning is finished and done with when the setting is completed. That is equally true of monetary co-operation.

The present predicament of Western Europe (pp. 66-7 above) calls for a more sustained and systematic planning. The vast arrears of maintenance, extension, and improvement of capital equipment give industry a quite exceptional degree of freedom in shaping its future and initiating new departures of all kinds. To leave the task to private enterprise would be to trust the economic fate of Western Europe to the haphazards of trial and error, under conditions where the margin of error has been disproportionately widened by uncertainties of all kinds.

In quiet times every trader takes existing demand as the starting point for his estimates of prospects. When a producer incurs expenditure on the upkeep, renewals, and improvements of his plant, it is in the expectation that the demand for his product will continue undiminished; when he extends his plant it is in the expectation that demand will expand. There are miscalculations and disappointments, but only within a relatively narrow margin, so long as there is a *continuity* of conditions.

Even new industries, which have to forecast demand for new products, are better placed to do so when the demand for existing products is pursuing an equable course and free markets reveal its tendencies.

The war, to say nothing of the preceding economic upheaval, has precipitated a huge and baffling discontinuity, to which the demand for different products is far from having adjusted itself. Producers find the demand for their products on the one hand stimulated by shortage and by inflation; on the other, restrained by controls at home and by import restrictions abroad. In the swirl of contrary currents they are at a loss how to steer.

A public authority, commissioned to take a wide view, and equipped with governmental channels of intelligence, is better placed than any one trading concern to forecast the community's needs for a product. If capital outlay is regulated by licensing, by allocation of materials, and by control of capital issues, something can be done towards bringing the future capacity of each industry into conformity with the forecast of the demand for its product.

The forecasts made by governmental authorities are not infallible, but they at any rate set out to take a total view instead of the limited and fragmentary view to which the individual trader is confined. And they can allow for considerations of public policy outside the cognizance of the individual trader, such as the balance of payments, the war potential, and the social and strategic aspects of the location of industry.

Planning in this sense places a heavy responsibility upon the Government, and it is hardly necessary to say that doubts are freely expressed in many quarters of the competence of any Government to undertake it. Whether these doubts are well founded it would be foreign to our present purpose to inquire. If Western Europe were relegating its economic life to the unimpeded rule of let-do, economic co-operation would be confined to agreements among privately owned concerns (so far as not prohibited as being in restraint of trade); it would hardly enter into projects for Western European Union. But we are a long way from that condition of things. The prevalence of planning in Western Europe, be it well or ill conceived, is a fact, which our study must accept.

Economic planning takes effect in government interference, but there are several degrees of interference. The classic instance of planning is the succession of Russian Five-Year Plans, which started in 1928. The Soviet Union Government had taken the entire industry of the country into its own hands, and the Five-Year Plans embodied its intentions in using the power which it had thus assumed. Nationalized industries in Western Europe are amenable to the same kind of planning. But here there is a complication, in that an industry which is nationalized in one country remains in the hands of private enterprise in another. The nationalized industry will be obedient to the directions of its own government, but co-operation between the two must be accommodated to the kind of planning which can be applied to the other.

Where private enterprise prevails, planning need not necessarily be imposed by coercive regulation. A Government which prepares a competent plan has something to offer to industry, and the industrialists may be persuaded that to go a long way in conformity with the plan is quite in accordance with their own interests. The government plan may be seen to fill in various gaps in the calculations on which the industrialists' projects are based. And if all the industries of the country are guided by the plan, each will be in a better position to judge what the others are doing. Nationalized industries of course fit quite naturally into such a scheme, and may facilitate its operation by acting as bell-wethers of the flock.

There are limits to what can be done by voluntary co-operation of private enterprise in governmental plans. Not only may the plans come into conflict with the direct interests of the industrial and commercial concerns, but there may be differences of opinion as to what the aims of public policy should be. And even when representatives of an industry agree to a plan, the refusal of a few to accept the decision may provoke or drive the majority to go back on it.

Planning therefore, if it is to be systematic, is likely to involve some legally enforceable regulation. Planning is chiefly concerned with long-term enterprise and therefore with the production and installation of capital equipment. It is in these that relatively permanent commitments are incurred by industry, and it is these therefore that must be subjected to controls.

International co-operation in economic planning would cover both the voluntary and the compulsory conformity of private enterprise to the plans. It would no doubt be limited to those parts of public policy in which the interests of the co-operating nations in some way overlap, or conflict, or are mutually dependent; it need not be overburdened by bringing in matters which can be satisfactorily settled by each nation for itself.

PLANNING AND THE BALANCE OF PAYMENTS

The nature and extent of Western European economic co-operation will depend on the common purposes of public policy to be aimed at. Conspicuous among these will be the balance of payments. With the short-period aspects of an adverse balance we have already dealt (pp. 55-65). But the anxieties of the present day are not confined to the short period.

The Committee of European Economic Co-operation said (General Report, Vol. 1, para. 30) that, while there would still be a large deficit in the balance of payments of the sixteen nations which it represented in the years following 1948, 'the purpose of the European Recovery Programme is to reduce this deficit as fast as possible. There will be some deficit in 1951; the participating countries have always depended on dollar earnings from the rest of the world to meet their deficit with the American Continent, and will do so in future. But by the end of 1951, given reasonably favourable external conditions, the deficit should be of dimensions which will be manageable through normal means without special aid.'

The programme did not extend beyond the end of 1951, and the estimated balance for the year 1951 still showed a deficit. Imports from the American Continent in that year were put at $8,182 million (Appendix D, p. 67), whereas exports to the American Continent were put at $3,945 million. An unfavourable balance of $325 million on invisible account would bring the deficit to $4,562 million. If there were a 'progressive reduction in the price of imports in relation to the price of exports', this deficit might be reduced to $3,540 million. Against this was to be set a surplus of exports in trade with non-participating countries outside the American Continent estimated at $640 million (or, if the price of imports fell, $1,142 million).

That would be a long way from a true balance with the Americas or even with the outside world as a whole. But the

Committee did not venture on any estimates for 1952 or subsequent years. The Committee's estimates were extremely conjectural. The O.E.E.C. in a recent report have made estimates for 1952 which show a substantial deficiency for the Continental countries of Western Europe. At any rate it cannot be assumed as certain that Western Europe will be able to eliminate its adverse balance, consistently with the conditions assumed, after 1951. It may do better than has been estimated, but, if it may do worse, the latter alternative cannot be disregarded.

When we say that American aid is needed in the years up to 1951, to fill the capital deficiency from which Western Europe is suffering, what we really mean is that the *current savings* of Western Europe are insufficient, and have to be supplemented from the current savings of the United States. But when fears are expressed that Western Europe will still be suffering from an ineradicable adverse balance after 1951, what is envisaged is not a continuing shortage of current savings, but an inability to procure indispensable imports. It is not forgotten, of course, that the economic progress of any country may be retarded by a deficiency of current savings, or that its progress may be assisted by an inflow of funds derived from the current savings of other countries. But the menace apprehended is different: it is that Western Europe will be unable to obtain the food for its subsistence, or the materials for its industry, from any quarter.

The question is one of area and population. The nations participating in the European Recovery Programme (exclusive of Greece and Turkey) have to support 242 millions of inhabitants in an area of one million square miles. The United States with less than three-fifths of the population has three times the area. The density of population in Western Europe is thus five times that in the United States, and greatly exceeds what would be compatible with self-sufficiency in the organic products of the land. To any human community the need for an adequate supply of these products is paramount. Western Europe therefore must in the future face the necessity of procuring a hard core of indispensable imports.

Some of the sources formerly available are likely to be either cut off or reduced in productivity. The produce of Eastern Europe tends to be diverted to the Soviet Union. The European dependencies in South East Asia, which used to sell materials to the United States, and to pass on most of the dollars thereby procured, either in payment for European exports of manufactures, or in the form of profits to European shareholders and traders, have suffered gravely from devastation and political disturbance. And there is in the countries which have hitherto been exporters of natural products a very widespread disposition to promote and encourage industrialization, to the detriment of those highly industrialized countries which need to obtain the means of paying for natural products by selling manufactured products.

Is there not a danger that Western Europe may find grave difficulty in procuring the indispensable supplies of natural products, both staple foodstuffs and materials of industry? The fear is that areas which used to import manufactured products and provided the means of paying for them by exporting surpluses of natural products, will become self-supporting; that they will produce all the manufactures they need, and, either through an increase in population or through a rise in their standard of living, will consume their natural products at home.

The picture is really one of world scarcity. The open spaces fill up, and all their produce is needed for their own inhabitants, so that nothing is left over for over-populated Western Europe. Without following out an extravagant hypothesis, we may yet suppose it possible that the industrialization of some countries, and the political isolation of others may so reduce the absorptive capacity of markets for exported manufactures, that the highly industrialized countries cannot obtain the natural products they need. They may be faced with the choice of forcing out exports or doing without imports which are deemed indispensable.

Would joint planning provide a remedy? It is possible that the countries of Western Europe could do more with a combined export drive than separately. An export drive which is thought to be the only means of procuring indispensable imports, is apt to culminate in pressing the sale on unfavourable terms of goods which are not fitted for foreign markets. A combined export drive can at least apply a uniform standard of fitness or unfitness, so that some of the co-operating countries do not incur heavier losses than others on this account, and the worst cases of unfitness are avoided. Combined action may produce plans for strengthening particular industries, for instance by standardization, by new forms of specialization, by exchange of information about processes, about sources of supply of materials, or about markets. Facilities may be created for mass production. In all such plans Governments can take the initiative, and there is a presumption that whatever is done to strengthen the competitive power of export industries will be in the interest of the particular concerns engaged in them.

NEW AND EXTENDED INDUSTRIES

This applies not only to export industries, but also to industries supplying the home market in competition with imports. New industries may be started in both categories. The planning of new or extended industries is already being started. And here we may quote a contribution from one of our number.

One of the greatest needs of Europe today is that Western Europe should become less dependent upon overseas imports of cereals. The Food and Agriculture Committee of the O.E.E.C. is, therefore, giving great attention to the steps which could be taken by the participating countries to increase their own production of cereals and feeding stuffs. On the theory that the most efficient way quickly to increase the production of cereals is not to bring in new areas of supply, but rather to bring to their maximum production existing areas of supply, it is likely that a serious endeavour will be made to make it possible for France to export by 1952 say, one million tons of wheat. If this is to be achieved it is not merely a question of providing France with the agricultural equipment, such as combines, tractors, balers, etc., but also a question of considering the supply of fertilizer, and the control of plant diseases, the suitability of seed types, and the provision of guaranteed markets for the disposal of any exportable surplus.

Another instance of a particular problem which calls both for joint planning and common action is oil. Almost all the countries in Western Europe plan to use greatly increased quantities of oil over the next few years and if they are to do so will have to extend their existing refinery capacity. Two problems arise. The first is to examine whether the existing oil installations are being put to the most economic use. For instance, it might be possible, by importing more crude oil into France and working the refineries there to their full capacity, to produce some refined products required by a number of countries in Europe, which at the present moment are being imported from the United States for dollars. Second, in the light of the examination made about existing refinery capacity and its utilization to agree what new refineries should be erected and where they should be located.

The chemical industry furnishes another example. There is no indigenous production of carbon black in Western Europe and the whole of its tire industry, therefore, depends upon imports of this chemical from the United States. Plans for the erection of European plants are now being made and the question arises of arranging the best intra-European distribution of the new product. Nitrogen and potash are also substances in short supply, the increased production of which in Europe would not only contribute to a saving in dollars, but would also greatly facilitate the increased production of cereals and feeding stuffs, which in turn would produce a further saving of dollars. Sulphur is another commodity in short supply, the production of which in Europe could be increased, if the existing mines were to be modernized and if new marketing arrangements could be made.

Western Europe is still short of rail transport equipment. On the other hand the potential productive capacity of freight cars and loco-motives is high and there is scope for a replanning of the production and export plans of the various manufacturing countries which, if successfully carried out, would enable Europe to be independent of American and Canadian imports. A similar position exists in regard to the production of motor trucks. There is good reason to think that Europe need today import no motor lorries from the Western Hemis-phere provided the existing capacity for this type of vehicle is put to the best use.

Timber, particularly softwood, remains in short supply, larger supplies of it being badly required both for pit props and as pulp for paper. A great deal of work has already been done to ensure that the timber import programmes of the Western European countries are drawn up after consultation and in regard to all the circumstances of each of the importing countries. Steps have already been taken to increase the production of timber in Germany and, as a result of consultation between the coal and timber experts of the Marshall Plan countries, further supplies of Scandinavian timber have been made available as larger supplies of coal have enabled the producing countries to reduce their consumption of wood as fuel. Furthermore, discussions have taken place, and are planned for the future, as a result of which increased supplies of the materials needed for logging operations, saw mills, tractors, etc., will be made available from within Europe for the countries in need of such supplies.

Coal and coke have for many months been substances whose produc-tion and distribution in Europe have been determined by international agreement, nor has the co-operative effort of the countries concerned ended there. The amount of mining machinery required by the various producers has been assessed, and as a result orders have been placed among the producers of it which have had the effect of greatly reducing the import of these materials from the Western Hemisphere.

Closely allied with the work of the Coal and Coke Committee is that done by the Steel Committee, the common action of the two Committees permitting the coal and coke supplies of Europe to be directed to the centres of steel and pig iron production so that the existing facilities for steel production can be put to greater and more efficient use. A further feature of the work of this Committee is the examination of the present output of all types of steel and by comparing this output with the needs of European industry for steel to see whether, if a surplus exists in one country of a particular type and an import requirement of that type figures in the overseas import programme of another country, it is possible to marry the surplus of the one country with the deficit of the other with the object of saving dollars. Apart from this day-to-day activity, the meetings of the Steel Committee permit a discussion of the longer term development plans of each of the main steel producing countries, as a result of which it should be possible to avoid duplication and the establishment of certain types of new and competing capacity.

The plans of the various European countries for the development of some of their overseas territories provide a fruitful field for further co-operative effort. The plans for the greater production of groundnuts in French West Africa give rise to problems of transport which can only be solved by agreement between the French and British authorities in West Africa, since much of what is produced has to be evacuated through British railways and ports whose present capacity is already strained.

The cattle industry also affords a field for joint action. One of the largest items in the combined import programme of Western Europe from the Western Hemisphere is the importation of meat. Whilst it is clearly impossible quickly to develop in West Africa a cattle industry on a scale comparable to that of Argentina, it is probable that a larger cattle industry could be built up in the West African highlands, if the necessary administrative arrangements could be agreed between the various Colonial authorities there and the present restrictions which prevent the movement of cattle across frontiers could be removed.

The Administration of the Dutch East Indies are at present engaged in an intensive programme of rehabilitation and of the development of new products. A very large part of the finished goods and machinery required for this programme has hitherto had to be obtained by the

Dutch Authorities from the United States. Examination of the detailed imports required has shown, however, that a substantial proportion of what is required could in future be supplied from Europe if the necessary arrangements could be made.

A somewhat similar problem arises in the metropolitan territories of a number of the participating countries in regard to agricultural machinery. The demand is presently in excess of the supply, but under the terms of the E.C.A. Act only a small part of the deficit can be obtained from the United States, since under that Act the export of agricultural machinery to Europe is limited to an annual amount of $75 million. Urgent consideration is, therefore, being given to the manufacture of the farm machinery in those countries where the industrial experience and facilities exist for the manufacture of what in some cases is rather complicated equipment.

In all such plans regard should be had to *cost*. We have seen how the existing problem of adverse balances arises from public policy demanding a volume of imports in excess of what exports, if left to the operation of free markets and competitive prices and rates of exchange, can pay for (above, pp. 55-8). If recourse is had to an export drive to bring the accruing foreign exchange up to the equivalent of the imports judged indispensable, it may be that the marginal exports are ill suited to their market, and can only be disposed of on extremely unfavourable terms in relation to their cost. In deciding whether a new or extended industry, which is destined to replace imports by home products, will help in solving the balance of payments problem, the cost involved, in terms of productive resources, should be weighed against the cost of marginal exports which would otherwise be necessary.

But of course the aim of the efforts now being made is to place Western Europe in a position of such economic strength as to procure the imports it needs *without strain*. If in the future any export drive is necessary, it should stop short of forcing out marginal exports at excessive cost. Imports in fact should not be limited to the hard core; there should be marginal imports to balance the marginal exports, and any which could not cover costs should be dispensed with.

That does not mean that Governments should necessarily leave the balance of payments to the free play of let-do, and wash their hands of it. Whatever they elect to do by way of planning or of influencing production or consumption would be reflected in their external trade policy.

Even though no restrictive import control may be necessary, bulk purchases of some essential supplies by governmental agencies may nevertheless be deemed desirable. And if bulk purchases are desirable at all, co-ordinated action by the purchasing Governments would evidently be an advantage.

DEFENCE AND THE LOCATION OF INDUSTRY

The easier the future balance of payments position of Western Europe, the less will be the need of government interference and supervision, and the less therefore the scope for international co-operation. On the other hand co-operation in defence will always call for some consequential economic co-operation. Every nation which aspires to military power must have regard to its sources of supply in time of war. Western Europe is irretrievably dependent on oversea supplies of food and materials, and all defence plans must safeguard these supplies. There must be the necessary shipping and aircraft and installations, and the armaments must include adequate sea and air power.

Defence plans must provide for the development of each country's war potential: on one side the mobilization of its forces, on the other the adaptation of its industry to war purposes. Economic policy in time of peace must secure the maintenance of those industries which are easily adaptable, some perhaps which are indispensable for certain categories of war supplies.

Economic co-operation would enable these measures of preparedness and adaptation to be taken for Western Europe as a unit, without regard to frontiers. Given the necessary pre-requisite of secure sea communications, co-operation in these respects can be extended across the Atlantic, and the war potential of Western Europe, the United States and Canada concerted, as was the actual war effort by the Combined Boards of the Second World War.

Closely allied to the war potential of Western Europe is the question of the location of industry. The location of industry cannot be dictated by strategic considerations; limits are placed on what is practicable by the existing communications and residential accommodation. But under existing post-war conditions the exceptional amount of new development to be undertaken allows room for strategic planning.

The location of industry is a part of the wider question of the distribution of population. This in turn raises the question of the application of aliens legislation by the countries of Western Europe to one another's nationals. A federation would presumably mean a common nationality for the people of all the federating States, and unrestricted movement and migration from one to another. And even without federation the co-operating nations might enter into agreements to that effect.

Unrestricted migration does not necessarily mean any greatly increased transfers of population. The obstacles of language and social ties and habits would remain. Nevertheless migration might occur. Differences in the standard of living or in opportunities of employment might in certain instances exert so powerful an attractive force as to overcome these obstacles. Whether migration so caused would be desirable or not depends on conflicting considerations. An evening out of differences in the standard of living would seem in itself desirable. Yet it would surely arouse strenuous opposition from all the communities threatened with a levelling down through an influx of immigrants. A mixture of human stocks in such communities might in some respects be regarded as beneficial; yet much might be lost through the severing of cultures and traditions which could only be preserved with the pure strains in which they have originated and grown.

The Treaty of Brussels foreshadows the conclusion of conventions 'in the sphere of social security' (Article II). If migration means the loss of accrued rights to benefits, that is a serious barrier. A completely unified system of social security would be hard to work unless money units were reliably convertible into one another. But something less than a unified system might provide for immigrants starting with accrued credits appropriate to age, and for a settlement of accounts between administrations on the basis of the liability each has been relieved of, actuarially calculated.

Part III
ORGANS OF CO-OPERATION

FEDERATION: POLITICAL OBJECTIONS

THE preceding sections have surveyed the field for co-operation under the two heads, military and economic. By what organs can co-operation best be put into effect?

We have seen that there is no possibility of a formal federation of Western Europe being immediately established. Are we to look forward to such a federation coming into being a few years hence as the culmination of the existing movement towards closer union?

Federation, it is said, would ride rough-shod over sentiments deeply rooted in history. It involves some definite limitation of sovereignty. Sovereignty is a technical term which may mean little to the popular mind. But when a limitation of sovereignty means a subjection of the monarchy to a Western European federal executive, or a loss of the identity of the Royal Navy in a Western European marine, the ordinary man may feel the ground trembling under his feet.

On the other hand supporters of federation might contend that a wider and deeper reading of history would go back to a past when national pride and aspiration had not taken shape, when all Christendom could be marshalled in a Crusade, or further back, when the vitality of the Western Empire was demonstrated by the Carolingian revival.

Without dwelling too much on such imaginings, we must turn to the circumstances of the present day.

Formal federation would bring into contact profoundly different political methods and traditions. Democracy works well in Great Britain. Though it often departs from the simplicity of a two-party alignment, parties are always so far dominated by the issues of the day that there is a line of cleavage between supporters of the Government and the opposition. An election decides the fate of the government, and stable governments are usual. Party splits, such as destroy a government's majority during the life of a Parliament, are relatively rare.

In the continental countries of Western Europe there is always a multiplicity of parties, which electoral systems calculated to secure minority representation tend to perpetuate. Frequently there is either a coalition Government or a Government dependent for its majority on a combination of parties. Where parties give or withhold support by reference to the issues calling for practical decision, parliamentary Government may work in much the same way as in Great Britain. But the parties are prone to insist too much on doctrinaire principles. When each party stipulates for measures which will mark progress towards its own particular ideal polity, as a condition of its support for those which its members are well aware are immediately necessary, the Government may be fatally weakened. In extreme cases intransigent parties stand in the way of the formation of *any* Government; that was the predicament which gave Mussolini his opportunity in 1922, when the march on Rome marked the breakdown of democracy, and opened the way to twenty years of dictatorship.

It is sometimes contended that a federal Parliament would be immune from the entanglements of party politics if their functions were strictly confined to the defence of the union. The common services need not include a customs union, for example, or a monetary union. But the implications of defence are so far-reaching that political issues are certain to arise. A merger of armed forces would confer on the federal authority:

(a) the ultimate responsibility for enforcing law and order;
(b) the power of assessing and exacting financial contributions;
(c) the power of determining and enforcing compulsory service;
(d) the direction of industry and commerce in conformity with military and strategic considerations;
(e) foreign policy, so far as it depends on military power.

The financial power must almost inevitably be a direct taxing power, the exercise of which will raise momentous political controversies as to the equitable distribution of fiscal burdens among the people. The assessment of a global contribution on each member State is liable to break down, not merely through dissatisfied member States actually refusing to accept their assessments, but through negligence or passive resistance resulting in crippling delays in making payment. And even the assessment of global contributions cannot be dissociated from the controversies as to the equitable distribution of burdens among classes and individuals.

The exigencies of total war make the political implications of the direction of industry and commerce by a defence authority, even in peace time, more serious and more controversial than they have been in the past. War-time controls and powers of requisition and direction in effect place the entire productive resources of a country at the disposal of its Government, the residue of free private enterprise being tolerated only at the Government's discretion. Peace-time preparedness requires that the way be kept open to bring the controls smoothly into operation. The defence authority must be in a position at all times to prevent by an over-riding legislative power any development in the economic structure of a member State which is likely to be inimical to this process. The local distribution of industries within the federation must conform to strategic requirements, and the adequate development of those industries on which the war potential depends must be ensured by an appropriate economic policy.

Of foreign policy it may be said that power is always present in the background. There are many international negotiations where bargaining is a matter of offering acceptable equivalents without reference to the relative power of the parties. But these as a rule are not properly matters of *policy*. A country's foreign policy is concerned with its relations of friendliness or the reverse with other countries, with the advantages it may obtain from them whether by inducement or by pressure, and with what it may itself be induced or compelled to give up.

If the members of a federation, while surrendering the responsibility for defence to the federal authority, retain their foreign policy in their own hands, they will find themselves from time to time engaged in negotiations in which they must rely upon an assured backing from the federal authority to enable them to stand up to the other parties. And in any case defence includes not only military alliances, but all those relations with countries potentially neutral, by which economic warfare would be affected. Peace-time trade treaties ought to be so framed as not to stand in the way of such restrictions as it may be desirable to apply in wartime in order to influence the economic relations of neutrals with an enemy.

In the days when alliances were dynastic, foreign policy had little contact with domestic affairs, so long as peace was maintained. But when the grouping of the Powers comes to be influenced by ideological aims, the contact becomes close. That was the effect of the wars of religion in the sixteenth and seventeenth centuries, and likewise of the grouping of the liberal and reactionary Powers after 1815. At the present time not only is communism in its totalitarian form the principal international issue, but Governments dependent on Socialist or Catholic parties favour close relations with other countries of similar political colour.

A Western European federation, therefore, even if limited to the purposes of defence, would offer a wide field for political forces in which the political methods and practices of the member States would find scope. The federal executive would be a powerful political instrument democratically constituted. And the very question of *extending* its powers would at all times be a matter of active political controversy. The political life of the members would be overshadowed by that of the centre, and would be more and more parochialized.

If democracy has in some countries fallen into discredit, the principal cause is that it does not work smoothly in the hands of intransigent parties. There is a danger that a European federation would be troubled not only by the intractability of some of the parties which take part in the political life of the Continent, but also by party divisions following lines of nationality. It is not to be assumed that a representative Assembly of Western Europe would produce a majority for the policies which the advocates of formal federation regard as the essential object of European Union. A directly elected Assembly dominated by representatives of France, Italy and the traditional neutrals might be so intent on expensive plans of social improvement that they would grudge funds for armaments, and would prefer a policy of detachment from a world struggle. A body composed not of directly elected representatives but of delegates from Governments would not be so irresponsible. But even they would not be immune, and, if they took decisions by a majority, there would be no certainty that the Governments favouring a firm policy would not be overruled.

In any case a federal legislature composed exclusively of

government delegates would not satisfy the aspirations of those who put their faith in formal federation. Such a body would accept national divisions as permanent, whereas a directly elected Assembly would at any rate hold out some hope of superseding them, by evolving party issues which divide all or most of the national electorates.

Western European Union is conceived as an association for defence of democratic institutions. If the object is identified with defence against communism, that is not because the democratic nations seek a defence against collectivism as an economic system. Socialism may culminate in a sweeping nationalization of the means of production, distribution, and exchange, and the collectivization of enterprise, without suppressing democracy. Undoubtedly many people would deplore the elimination of profit-making private enterprise, but the menace against which defence is demanded is not of mere collectivism but of collectivism founded upon totalitarian terrorism.

Projects of Western European Union all presuppose that the nations to be associated together will remain democratic. It has been pointed out above (pp. 24-6) that in more than one of them the political situation is insecure.

Advocates of formal federation may claim that a federal constitution, firmly founded on a democratic franchise throughout its territory, would be a safeguard against a lapse from democracy on the part of any of its component States, and it is said that French opinion tends to advocate a federation as a safeguard against a political relapse of Germany.

Is that claim tenable? Federation would not by itself prevent the establishment of a dictatorship in one of the States. The forms of democratic election for the representative chamber of the federal legislature might be a constitutional requirement, but nowadays dictatorships have no difficulty in maintaining the forms, so long as they can exclude all opposition candidates from nomination. The resources of the dictator's country for war, in wealth and manpower, would, it is true, be under the control not of the dictator, but of the federation. But on the assumption that the dictatorship could not be brought to an end by persuasion or pressure, the position of the federation would be gravely prejudiced: either the dictator's country would have to be excluded from it (whether by expulsion or by voluntary secession); or the dictatorship would continue to influence policy within it. Whether the dictatorship were communist or fascist in character, its presence in the counsels of the federation would be a continuing danger. Indeed the federation might not merely be weakened by dissensions but actually itself turned into a totalitarian system by the dictator's party gaining control of the federal executive.

Without building hypothesis on hypothesis, it will be enough to say that formal federation will not necessarily supply the best safeguard against lapses into totalitarian terrorism within Western Europe.

FEDERATION AND THE COMMONWEALTH

Even if the foregoing grounds were not held decisive against a formal federation, it would be impossible to reconcile the constitution of a united Western Europe in that shape with the continued existence of the British Commonwealth as now conceived. The Commonwealth is an association of co-equal autonomous nations linked together formally by a common citizenship and a common loyalty and informally by devotion to common ideals, the sharing of a common scale of values. The common loyalty is symbolized by the Crown, which, though bound by the observance of democratic constitutional practices, always remains a *reserve* of sovereign executive power in every Dominion. Here it is important to remember that the King is King of Canada, Australia, New Zealand, and South Africa, just as much as he is King of Great Britain.

The extension of Dominion status to India, Pakistan, and Ceylon has not essentially altered this conception of the Commonwealth. They are free (like the older Dominions) to leave the Commonwealth at any time. If they ceased to share in the loyalties, the ideals, and the scale of values on which the unity of the Commonwealth is founded, they would probably leave it as soon as the difference of outlook became apparent in any major practical issue.

If the United Kingdom were merged in a Western European federation, the federation could not replace it as a member of the Commonwealth. Even if the common citizenship were extended to include the entire membership of the federation and the Commonwealth, that would not of itself create between the Dominions and the federation the intangible links which now exist between the Dominions and the United Kingdom.

Constitutionally the adhesion of the United Kingdom to a federation would have the effect of mediatizing the British Crown, as the creation of the German Empire mediatized the Kings, Grand Dukes, and Dukes who had previously enjoyed independence. It is to the Crown that every British subject (or citizen) owes his allegiance. But the creation of a European super-state, of which Britain was a constituent part, would fundamentally alter this position. A Canadian or New Zealander or Jamaican would still owe undivided allegiance to the Crown. But a British subject in the United Kingdom would be differently placed. He would still owe allegiance to the King but only subject to the overriding duty to the Federal Executive and Legislature of United Europe.

In matters of war and peace, foreign policy, and defence, the Dominions retain their independence. In that respect the absorption of the United Kingdom into a federation would make no formal difference. Yet the practice by which the Government of the United Kingdom keeps in touch with the Dominions in shaping both its foreign policy and its defence policy could not fail to be profoundly modified. The Government of the United Kingdom could not speak for the Government of the federation in these matters, while to the Dominions the Government of the federation would have the guise of an alien body, in which the British element could only take a subordinate part.

That the Dominions would at any time themselves become members of the federation is hardly conceivable. They would be surrendering that freedom of action in peace and war, foreign policy, and defence, which they have valued so highly since the Statute of Westminster assured it to them. Nor is it at all certain that the continental countries would welcome them. The Dominions, notwithstanding the large French-speaking population in Canada and the fact that the majority of the European population of the Union of South Africa is of Dutch descent, have relations with the European Continental countries considerably less close than those which either the former or the latter have with the United Kingdom. The adhesion of the Asian

Dominions would alter the whole conception of a European Union.

A JOINT COUNCIL

If formal federation in course of time is not to be the aim, what is left? Some of the proposals discussed above will be ruled out on the ground that they are bound to lead to formal federation: for examples, a merger of armaments, a customs union, a common currency.

Every country therefore will retain undivided authority over its forces, its budget, and its monetary policy. No individual will have to submit to any governmental authority other than those of his own country. Whatever concerted action is to be taken will be through the separate legislatures and executives of the co-operating countries.

In the absence of any federal constitution, decisions for concerted action must be taken by a body representing the participating Governments. The representative body might agree to take decisions by voting (voting power presumably being suitably weighted). Each Government would then be pledged to carry out the decisions, even if its representatives had voted in the minority.

That would be a substantial step in the direction of federation. But it would fail to secure some of the principal advantages of federation. The representative body would have no legislative powers, and, should legislation be required, the participating Governments could only undertake to *promote* it in their own legislatures; they could not pledge themselves to secure its enactment.

So long as only executive action was involved, the Governments could give directions to their own departments. But a body voting by majorities is not well fitted for executive action. It has not the same sense of responsibility as a hierarchical organization under a single head. When decisions forming an interconnected series have to be taken, it may not be possible to secure a consistent majority for all; there will be one set of dissentients for one, another set of dissentients for another; and the defeat of some may stultify the rest.

Consequently where the executive power of a nation is to be

in the hands not of a single individual, but of a council or cabinet, experience has shown unanimity to be the best working rule. But unanimity does not mean free resort to an obstructive veto. A Cabinet endeavours to meet the objections of its minority members, and the minority members themselves, faced with the alternatives of agreeing or breaking up the Government, will go far towards sinking their differences.

A council representing a group of co-operating nations is not exactly parallel to a cabinet governing one nation. When a Government breaks up, a new one is formed. The disruption of an international group amounts to a failure of its mission. If the member Governments regard co-operation as vitally important, they will approach their differences in the same spirit as a Cabinet devoted to a political cause. The requirement of unanimity means that any dissentient member is in a position to insist on concessions, but in practice, rather than risk disruption, the member will not push insistence to extremes.

The membership may include a fringe of lukewarm supporters, to whom co-operation is not at all vital, and who would try to obstruct unwelcome decisions, or to extort concessions by trading on their associates' unwillingness to break up the union. The inclusion of such members would be an inherent cause of weakness, whatever the constitution or the procedure of the union. The course of wisdom might be to refuse admission to the original membership of any to whom co-operation is not a real and dominant interest. That dominant interest will suffice to secure unanimity. On secondary matters the example of the O.E.E.C. might be followed, and dissenting members be allowed to contract out of a decision which remains binding on those accepting it. On the other hand, it may be judged essential to retain the adhesion of a waverer, who, if excluded, would forthwith succumb to communist influence. How far it would be wise to go in trying to prevent such a lapse would of course depend on the circumstances of the case. The danger of going too far is obvious.

But, it may be objected, will not unanimity inevitably be subject to the weaknesses of the 'Conference Method?' Not if the mutual trust of the members and their will to co-operate are strong enough.

CO-OPERATION IN THE COMMONWEALTH

Here something may be learnt from the political life of the British Commonwealth. The British Empire formerly consisted of the United Kingdom and its conquests and colonies—its 'Possessions.' The legislature of the United Kingdom had the overriding power of making laws for them all. The secession of the North American Colonies disclosed an inherent contradiction between the British institution of parliamentary government and the exercise of authority over a politically mature community overseas.

The lesson was learnt. As democratic communities grew up in the oversea colonies, responsible government was conferred upon them. Up to the time of the Statute of Westminster (1931) the overriding power of the legislature of the United Kingdom continued. But this power had fallen long before into disuse (at any rate in application to any firmly established Colonial or Dominion democracy).

The Statute of Westminster deprived the Empire of its governmental unity, but powerful unifying principles still remained. The King of Great Britain was still King of each Dominion. He ruled as a constitutional monarch, abstaining from any part in political decisions constitutionally reached, and, in the Dominions, even the formal authority or assent which a constitutional monarch gives was delegated to vicegerents. Nevertheless in the last resort the Government was the King's Government, the vicegerent was the Governor formally appointed by the King.

More immediately operative was the common citizenship of the entire Empire. The peoples of Dominions and Colonies and British India were all alike British subjects; those of other Dependencies were British protected persons. Palmerston is remembered as much for his pronouncement that an obscure trader from Gibraltar who could claim, *civis Britannicus sum*, would receive the full support of the Empire, as for anything in his political career.

The growth of responsible parliamentary government in the Dominions relieved the forces of the United Kingdom of the obligation of maintaining law and order in their territories, but not of the obligation to defend the Empire. Up to 1914 the contribution of the oversea Empire to defence had been quite subsidiary. Everything depended on British sea-power, and British sea-power depended on the British navy.

The first World War saw the Dominions participating in the British war effort on a great scale. That sole responsibility of the United Kingdom for defence, which had till then been one of the fundamental principles of unity, was at an end. In place of it was an imponderable joint responsibility, which the Statute of Westminster was expressly designed to free from any legally defined obligation.

The Commonwealth has been gradually divesting itself of the legal attributes of unity. The hegemony of the United Kingdom, as embodied in the overriding legislative power and the sole responsibility for defence, has been deliberately surrendered. And the logical consequence, the right of a Dominion to remain neutral when the United Kingdom is at war, has been accepted. Even the common monarchy is in question, and the common citizenship has been modified.

Yet the *will to co-operate* has survived. It has been expressed through something very like the 'Conference Method.' It is primarily in foreign policy that the need for co-operation is felt. Each Dominion has its own foreign policy, and in many matters the United Kingdom and they can take independent and different lines without affecting their fundamental unity of action. This was especially so so long as foreign policy was based on the League of Nations and Collective Security. Members of the League often had to make decisions in a judicial spirit. Where national interests were not involved, members of the Commonwealth could form their views independently.

The relapse of the world into power politics however has once more linked foreign policy closely to defence policy, and since 1935 the foreign policy of every member of the Commonwealth has had to be guided by reference to the potential appeal to force. Underlying the policy of all is the assumption that each must be able to rely on the moral approval and support of all the rest if the contingency of an appeal to force comes into sight. It is this vital consideration that ensures mutual consultation on all critical points of foreign policy. Concurrence of the members of the Commonwealth in one another's foreign policy and defence policy is therefore given with a full sense of responsibility.

The mutual trust that makes political co-operation possible leads on to economic co-operation. This has been mainly the spontaneous co-operation of private enterprise, taking shape in intimate commercial and financial relations, and in a free and active flow of capital within the Commonwealth. But the economic co-operation of the Commonwealth Governments has fallen quite naturally into place as the scope of governmental responsibility for economic life has been extended.

ORGANS OF UNION

The history of the Commonwealth has been one of a devolution of power from the centre to the circumference; the problem of Western European Union is one of a transfer in some degree of authority from the circumference to the centre. What is common to them is the essential need of mutual trust.

To recall how formidable are the obstacles in the way of mutual trust, it will be sufficient to refer to the passage on pp. 20-6 above. Yet we must assume that essential prerequisite to be fulfilled. Mutual trust once secured, a more clearly defined union than that of the Commonwealth would be in sight—more clearly defined because it would be needed to meet more immediate exigencies. Definite plans for defence must be made. Economic co-operation is imperative as a condition of American aid.

It is already established that consultation must be continuous, and that the organs of consultation must have permanent official bodies attached to them to plan concerted action. The staffs which make defence plans are a well-established institution, and a joint staff is an essential feature of a military alliance which aspires to be anything more than a gesture. The Defence Ministers of the five signatories of the Brussels Treaty form a Military Committee. There is a joint staff, and alongside it a Committee, with Lord Montgomery as Chairman, possessing some of the attributes of a joint command.

The organs of economic co-operation are still of a provisional character. The O.E.E.C. has been working under pressure to produce programmes immediately required as a basis for the administration and allocation of American aid. So far as the public are aware, the problem of joint planning has only been touched.

Much has been written from time to time about the need for an economic general staff as an organ of government. It would be the counterpart of a military general staff, to be entrusted with the making of economic plans, in the same way as a military general staff is entrusted with the making of defence plans. It would not be a merely advisory body, for it would make *constructive* plans fit to give direct and adequate instructions to the Departments responsible for administrative action. It would have the same kind of responsibility for the plans being reliable and practicable as a military staff has for a plan of campaign.

A military general staff has a specified objective referred to it, and proceeds to work out in detail the character and extent of the forces required, their disposition, and the contingencies to be provided against as the campaign develops. Consequential on these plans are the orders to be given for supplies, equipment, transport, etc., and all the administrative decisions to be made.

If the objective is adopted, the plans are at the disposal of the command. They are of course only operative to the extent that the command chooses. In a sense therefore the staff is only 'advisory'. But in practice the command has to rely on the staff as an essential part of its administrative system. An advisory body recommends what seems desirable. An administrative body specifies in detail the action to be taken for an appointed end. The members of the staff are assumed to be competent to do their work, like the members of a public department.

An economic general staff would similarly have an objective referred to it, and would have to consider all the measures required to put the policy embodied in it into effect. It would have to have the same sort of mastery of economic principles that a military staff has of strategy and tactics. Yet while a primary function of an economic general staff would be to foresee the economic consequences and repercussions of its plans, the plans would be *business* plans, and people conversant with business in its various branches, industry, commerce, transport, and finance, would be needed to join in preparing them. An economic general staff would no more be composed exclusively of economists than a military general staff of strategists.

A body so constituted would receive directions from whatever representative authority or joint council is created to decide the policy of Western Europe. Its task would be to apply the policy so defined from day to day, and its decisions, so long as they were within the scope of the directions and in accord with them, would be operative.

The actual administration of the services concerned would rest with the several Governments of the co-operating nations, but in general their departments would accept the decisions as equivalent to orders from their own authorities. Should the action to be taken by a Department need new legislation, it would be for the Government (at the instance of the Department) to procure the necessary measure from the legislature.

Here, it may be pointed out, is one of the fundamental differences between a formal federation and a lesser union. A federal legislature's enactments would be binding throughout the union, whereas the policy of a joint council, even after all the executive Governments had accepted it, might yet be rejected by one or more of the separate legislatures.

The difference is not wholly in favour of federation. If the rejection is based on serious grounds of opposition, the overriding of this opposition by a federal legislature may have a more disruptive effect than the rejection of the policy by a State legislature. If the preservation of the union is accepted by all parties in the State legislature as a paramount object, and if the policy involved is really important for that purpose, the rejection is not likely to be persisted in. If all the legislatures can be induced to accept the policy with its consequences, the policy will be the more firmly founded. A very great part of the work of the union staffs, military and economic, by which the joint council is to be served, would be administrative, not involving legislation.

Should the union staffs themselves have a representative character, or should the representation of the participating nations be exclusively concentrated in the joint council? Undoubtedly the staffs would have to keep closely in touch with the national Departments responsible for the carrying out of their decisions. A decision would sometimes be questioned by a member Government on the ground either that it did not conform to the true intentions of the joint council, or that the directions given would have consequences not previously foreseen, and ought to be reconsidered. Care and foresight in framing the directions, and in formulating the decisions, should reduce such questionings to a minimum. But there should also be continuing consultation with the national Departments concerned.

But to place a commission or board representative of all the nations at the head of the union staff would not necessarily be the best way of securing this end. What is wanted from the union staff is a technically sound plan (military or economic, as the case may be) to carry out an agreed policy. The union staff should be organized as a departmental hierarchy, recruited indifferently from the participating countries, appointments being made on grounds of personal fitness without regard to nationality.

The union staff has to make plans for carrying out the policy given to it. A plan will consist of directions to national Departments, specifying the action each is to take; for the union staff has no executive power of its own, and the national Departments are the only administrative bodies through which it can act.

The directions to be given to a Department must be referred to it in draft at the earliest stage, and must be wrought into shape by the Department and the union staff in collaboration. Only so can the directions given to each national department be adapted to the law and practice under which it is accustomed to work.

We would not rule out the possibility of this collaboration being secured by placing in authority, at the head of the union staff, a directorate composed of representatives of the participating countries. But it is possible that the number of countries might be such as to make a representative directorate cumbersome. And in any case it might be found that collaboration is best maintained at a level below the head, provided that the representatives of national Departments are of sufficient standing to have full cognisance of the questions of policy arising.

Should the plans made by the military and economic staffs come back to the joint council for confirmation? The joint council might adopt a resolution in general terms with very far-reaching effects, and could hardly give the union staff plenary powers to impose all the consequential directions on the national departments concerned, without giving the Ministers, who are responsible to their own parliaments, an opportunity to reconsider the policy in the light of the concrete plan. On the other hand, when a decision given by the joint council really is sufficient in itself to form the basis of practical action, a reference back to it of the union staff's plan at the stage when it is ready to be put into operation by the national Departments might be the occasion of delay and indecision.

If a plan came before the joint council for confirmation, every Government represented would proceed to refer it to those of its own Departments which would be responsible for carrying it out. Only after their comments had been received could the joint council signify its approval.

After that stage, it would be difficult for Departments to raise objections; so their examination of the plan would have to be thorough, and would take time. Yet even after the confirmation of the plan, unforeseen objections might arise. Confirmation therefore would not be really final.

Evidently a more expeditious procedure would be to pass the plan direct from the union staff to the national Departments, and to let them proceed to carry it out unless they raised any objections. Continuous consultation ought usually to anticipate objections, but if nevertheless any did emerge, and could not be surmounted at lower levels, they would have to come before the joint council.

It would not be necessary to follow the same procedure in all cases. Sometimes the joint council would find it desirable to enunciate a policy on very broad and general lines, to be worked out in detail by the union staff and the national Departments, and then to be brought up again for final confirmation. In other cases the best procedure might be for the union staff or one of the Governments to put up a proposal in sufficiently detailed form for the joint council to give it definitive approval. In any case it would at all times be open to any Government, a Department of which desired a modification of a plan previously approved, to bring an amending proposal before the joint council.

The foregoing remarks apply to the military and economic organizations of a Western European Union. Foreign policy would be on a somewhat different footing. Principles agreed on by the joint council could be applied without the intervention of an expert body corresponding to the military and economic union staffs. The foreign offices of the participating nations would brief their ministers for the meetings of the joint council, and the formulations of foreign policy, read with the briefs, would give them definite enough guidance.

Western European co-operation would extend into other fields. The preamble of the Treaty of Brussels includes the strengthening of the cultural ties by which the signatories are united, and under Article III they declare that they will 'make every effort in common to lead their peoples towards a better understanding of the principles which form the basis of their common civilization, and to promote cultural exchanges by conventions between themselves or by other means'. Our reference however was especially directed to the economic, political, and strategic aspects of the question, and it is these which have been most prominent in current discussions of it. We do not propose to pursue the question of cultural co-operation.

A WESTERN EUROPEAN ASSEMBLY

Several proposals have recently been made for the creation of an Assembly representing the nations of Western Europe. As was pointed out above (pp. 41 and 105), an assembly directly elected by the voters in the constituent countries is usually regarded as essential to a formal federation. But since the creation of such an assembly at an early date would hardly be feasible, supporters of federation have suggested that an assembly should be formed of members selected by the national parliaments. The proposal put before the Consultative Council in October 1948 by the French and Belgian Governments (above, p. 32) was so conceived. The Council decided at its January meeting that for matters other than defence there should be a Council of Europe composed of a ministerial committee, in which binding decisions could be reached, and of a Consultative Assembly. The membership of the latter would be selected by each Government in the manner suited to its own constitutional usage.

A Government would have free discretion either to choose members of its own Parliament, whether in proportion to party strength, or on any other principle, or to choose representatives partly or wholly from outside the political circle. It might choose them exclusively from its own supporters, but presumably they would speak and vote according to their individual convictions.

A Consultative Assembly is far from being a federal legislature. Nevertheless a Consultative Assembly which really reflects public opinion almost inevitably acquires power. The ministerial committee, which will represent the authority of Governments, could not be indifferent to the recommendations and protests of an assembly representing Parliaments.

The assembly now contemplated would not necessarily represent Parliaments. But in any case the members may be expected to be people of consequence, with sufficient independence to qualify as spokesmen of their fellow-countrymen.

Members chosen by a national Parliament, or by the Government by selection from the Parliament, might merely reflect existing party structure and add nothing to what was already known about public opinion.

Each party would no doubt tend to select as its representatives individuals known to be interested in the project of Western European Union. Those interested in the project are apt to be those favouring it, and a membership chosen on that principle might well give a distorted version of public opinion. Even a deliberate selection of some opponents and objectors to balance the supporters would not necessarily give a more faithful picture.

The most suitable representation would be composed of people who, whatever their views of the project might be, would accept the existence of Western European Union, with its actual structure, as a given fact, not to be questioned, and would be interested in the practical issues arising within that limitation.

As indicated above (p. 41-2) advocates of federation would regard an assembly of the kind now contemplated as a stepping stone to one directly elected by the voters themselves. Direct election would not infallibly secure a better result than election by Parliaments, for probably the candidates would be chosen and the issues formulated by party organizations. But direct election would offer a better opportunity of freeing the essential issues from these entanglements.

The objections stated above (pp. 101-8) to a formal federation are mainly British objections: the incompatibility of British political practices and habits with those of the Continent, and the impossibility of reconciling the preservation of the Commonwealth with the merger of the sovereignty of the United Kingdom in a federation. On the other hand a union formulating policy through a joint council representing Governments and working through union staffs would not conflict either with the spirit of British political life or with that of the Commonwealth. The Government of the United Kingdom would play its part in both the union and the Commonwealth.

COLONIES

The question of co-operation in the development of colonial resources (pp. 97-8 above) involves difficult constitutional problems. Members of the United Nations who are responsible for 'the administration of territories whose peoples have not yet attained a full measure of self-government . . . accept as a sacred trust the obligation to promote to the utmost . . . the well-being of the inhabitants of these territories', and to this end (b), 'to develop self-government, to take due account of the political aspirations of the peoples, and to assist them in the progressive development of their free political institutions, according to the particular circumstances of each territory and its peoples, and their varying stages of advancement' (Article 73).

This has for a generation or more been, ostensibly at any rate, the British policy, and it may be assumed that all the colonial Powers of Western Europe will hold themselves to be bound by it. They abjure despotic power over their dependencies, and will not claim freedom to direct the application of their colonial resources to suit either themselves or one another.

They undertake (article 73d) 'to promote constructive measures of development, to encourage research, and to co-operate with one another and, when and where appropriate, with specialized international bodies with a view to the practical achievement of the social, economic, and scientific purposes set forth in this Article'. Thus the colonial Powers are to promote constructive measures of development and to co-operate with one another in doing so. Western Europe includes the most important colonial Powers, so that co-operation among them does not fall far short of co-operation throughout the membership of the United Nations.

Western European Union need not necessarily encroach on the exclusive responsibility of each for its own dependencies. Each will carry out through its own executive and legislative power whatever is agreed upon with the others in regard to colonial resources.

If Article 73 is to be respected, nothing will be agreed upon which would conflict with the prior claim of the welfare of the inhabitants. But, within the limits set by that condition, there will always be some choice as to the nature and direction of development.

Economic development leads up to the production of something to be *sold*. The interests of those who buy are concerned as well as of those who produce.

There are colonies which are overpopulated, and for which industrialization holds out the best prospect of an improved standard of living. Industrialization of a colony may be in direct conflict with the interests of Western Europe: it may supplant European manufactured exports, and absorb the colony's former exportable surplus of materials and foodstuffs in its own people's expanded demand. The attitude of the metropolitan country towards these problems is too far-reaching a question to be explored in the present connexion. But it may be pointed out that the densely populated colonies of Asia, where industrialization is most likely to be recommended, are those where the demand for self-government is most insistent. The decision may be taken out of the metropolitan countries' hands.

Development of the more sparsely populated colonies (chiefly those of Africa) is naturally more in the direction of increased output of foodstuffs and materials. It may be plausibly argued that the interests of the colonial Powers and of their colonies are here at one. The markets for the colonies' products are bound to be mainly in Europe and America, and their interests will be best served if their development is so planned as to suit the needs of these markets,

The capital funds required for development will probably have to be provided by the metropolitan Governments rather than by private enterprise. In so far as that is so, the Governments will be in a position to choose what the products for which development is destined shall be. Co-operation among the metropolitan Governments means that in making this choice the potentialities of the colonies can be treated as one whole.

Each of the colonial Powers has its own chosen policy, and they would almost certainly see insuperable objections to handing over their dependencies to a single authority. Even a federation of Western Europe need not necessarily have a single colonial administration. Each of the federating States might retain its own colonies. But if the federation had a customs union, the question of preferential duties on colonial products would presumably be one for the federal legislature.

Every country assumes the responsibility for the defence of its own colonies. If the general responsibility for defence is transferred to a federation, the specific responsibility for the defence of the colonies goes with it. Both the defence of each colony against attack and the contribution of each colony to the defence of the federation become the concern of the federal executive and legislature. Where co-operation in defence is secured by a union less close than federation, and each country retains control over its own forces, a common colonial defence policy will be agreed upon through the joint council and the military staffs which assist it. In devising a colonial defence policy, whether for a single colonial Power, or for a union or federation of Western Europe, the separate interests of the colonial peoples must be taken into consideration. They may care nothing for the quarrels in which Western Europe may be involved. They may prefer to remain defenceless; the worst that could happen would be a change of masters, and in their eyes a change might be for the better.

On the other hand, Article 73 of the Charter is expressly limited by the qualification, 'within the system of international peace and security established by the present Charter', and under Article 43, 'all members of the United Nations, in order to contribute to the maintenance of international peace and security, undertake to make available to the Security Council' armed forces, etc., as agreed. It would seem to be quite in accordance with the Charter that a colony should contribute something under Article 43. The agreement to that effect could only be through the metropolitan country, so that the colonial Powers of Western Europe would be responsible to the Security Council for the forces and warlike supplies of their colonies.

That does not necessarily mean placing a share of the burden of armaments upon the colonies. The metropolitan country may pay the cost. If it is in any case subsidizing a colony, it obviously will not ask for a financial contribution (though the subsidy may be reduced below what would otherwise have been granted). But even so the actual manpower and supplies provided by the colony may be an important reinforcement.

Colonies may also give valuable facilities in the shape of bases and strategic points, lines of transport and communication, ports, airports, etc.

If the issue is not one of enforcement of the decisions of the Security Council, but of collective self-defence under Article 51 of the Charter, the case for calling upon the manpower and resources of the colonies is not so clear. The metropolitan country and its colonies are under a single sovereignty, and it may be argued that an attack on any part of the territory governed by it is an attack on the whole, and justifies defence by the whole. On the other hand Article 73 overrides the conception of a single indivisible sovereignty. It distinguishes the duties and functions of the sovereign Power in the exercise of authority over a colony from its duties and functions in the exercise of authority over the metropolitan country.

A country involved in actual war is not likely to let any consideration of trusteeship stand in the way of making the utmost use of colonial resources under its jurisdiction. It will claim that collective self-defence is in the true interest of the colonial peoples, and will not listen to any arguments to the contrary.

In time of peace it cannot afford to be so assertive; it must be prepared to defend its proceedings from the standpoint of Article 73. Perhaps the simple solution of the problem lies in the circumstance that, when the metropolitan country is at war, international law regards the colonies as *ipso facto* involved in the same state of war. And if they are at war they must be prepared to defend themselves.

CONCLUSION

THE peoples of Western Europe have been pinning their hopes of escape from their present troubles upon a closer union. Nevertheless it is not to be taken as axiomatic that a close union of Western Europe is either desirable or practicable. We indicated some of the difficulties and dangers in our introductory section, but we then accepted the position that the United Kingdom at any rate is committed to the policy of closer union in some form.

Even while our discussions have been in progress, events have followed one another quickly. The formation of our Group almost coincided in time with the coup of 25 February 1948 which established totalitarian rule in Czechoslovakia, and purged the Government of all non-communist members. Within a few weeks followed the Treaty of Brussels, and then the final enactment of the Economic Co-operation Act, confirming American aid to Europe. In the setting up of the Consultative Council under the Brussels Treaty and the Organization for European Economic Co-operation the first steps have been taken towards the embodiment of Western European Union in organs of co-operation.

In July 1948 began conversations on the subject of defence between the signatories of the Brussels Treaty on the one side and the United States and Canada on the other, so that a North Atlantic defence pact is coming into view, and the Scandinavian countries have engaged in negotiations on the subject of defence.

The big unofficial international conference at the Hague in May 1948, styled 'The Congress of Europe', and the subsequent meeting of members of Western European Parliaments at Interlaken, have led to the proposal for a Council of Europe, including a consultative Assembly (above pp. 33 and 117).

The announcement on 7 June, as the result of a Conference in London, that a Constituent Assembly representing the German States was to be convened to frame a Constitution for Germany, made the question of the inclusion of Germany in a Western European Union a practical issue.

These various moves have arisen out of the circumstances of the time. There are ends urgently sought, to which closer union appears to offer the means. But the approach to closer union is in great part an uncharted sea. Our Group has been taking soundings; here are shallows and the threat of shoals; there we have found the promise of a channel. But we do not ignore the possibility either of an undisclosed channel through the shallows or of an undisclosed barrier in what we have marked as a channel.

It is not a dead material world that we have been exploring, but living human nature. Human nature, with its habits, prejudices, and passions, is a perpetually changing medium. The obstacles we encounter are not immovable, like a rock or a shoal. They are products of the human will, and the human will is amenable to change. It may be changed not merely through one gust of passion being succeeded by another; it may yield to appeals to reason, provided the link between practicable means and desirable ends be made abundantly clear.

Questions of defence have figured prominently in our study. The peoples of the world have tried hard to rid themselves of power politics, and to establish collective security under the League of Nations or the United Nations Organization, but in present circumstances have to admit failure. The alienation of the communist States from the rest of the world has disappointed these hopes.

Militant communism has attained a preponderance of power in Europe. It is in the hope of securing themselves against that menace, and in the conviction that democratic political institutions are the best safeguard of individual liberty, that the democratic nations of Europe have been moved to form a closer union. They need a leadership of their combined effort to secure as effective a unity as the leadership of the communist party in the rival group; but the leadership must be on a democratic foundation.

A federal Government would be directly responsible to the peoples of the associated nations. We have pointed out difficulties in the way of formal federation, and have indicated alternative means of securing the close co-operation of the Associated Governments. Though our discussions seem clearly to point to a conclusion adverse to formal federation, we would by no means be dogmatic about it. The truest friend of any policy is he who warns its advocates of the difficulties in the way.

Recently the conception of Western European Union in defence has begun to merge in a wider conception of North Atlantic union. The same mechanism which we have suggested for the co-operation of Western European Governments with one another could equally provide for their co-operation with the United States and Canada.

This extension of co-operation in defence does not call for any modification of plans for economic co-operation, for the United States is already playing a leading part in the economic co-operation of Western Europe.

The Western nations have seen minority communist parties seizing power in those countries of Eastern Europe that have been overawed by the presence or proximity of Russian forces. Each of these strokes has been a *conquest* in the course of a veritable war, the 'class war' of the Communist Manifesto. If there are to be further conquests, each in turn will be an addition to the strength of militant communism and a subtraction from the strength of democracy and liberty. Western European Union is designed to offer a defence against further conquests. It is to assemble democratic forces as a counterpoise to militant communism, so that in the future no democratic country need be overawed.

That is the logic of events. But it is not to be assumed that the issue between communism and democracy is a conflict of national *interests*, in which one side hopes to make gains at the expense of the other. The difference is, ostensibly at any rate, one of opinion as to how human welfare and justice can best be promoted by economic and political institutions.

No worse method of settling the issue could be imagined than trial by battle. Undoubtedly the process by which dictatorships have been established in Eastern Europe has been in essence a resort to force. And dictatorships in the hands of fanatics who may commit their cause to war, in disregard of a desire for peace among their own peoples, are dangerous to peace. But the dictatorships exist, and, as things are, Europe must continue for a time to be divided.

It will be the course of wisdom to let time and experience test these political and economic systems. The establishment of a Western European Union and an Atlantic Pact affords the best hope of an interval of let-live, in which fear and fanaticism can subside. If the cause of democracy and liberty is securely founded on right reason and true values, it will come into its own. Mutual toleration will lead to mutual understanding. So, perhaps, can the state of crisis which is now shaking the world be brought to an end, and a catastrophe avoided.

A union for defence can do no more than give the world a breathing space. On a longer view, a closer union of Western Europe may yet make a great contribution to the future of mankind. It may be a model for the unified action of a group of sovereign States. If the schism which has been the occasion of its being set up is once healed, the union may be extended to embrace all Europe; and the conception of an association for collective self-defence may be superseded by that of a regional pact under the United Nations Charter.

Therefore the measures taken and to be taken towards closer union should be conceived not as expedients improvised to meet present dangers, but as steps towards a future in which the feuds and jealousies which have riven Europe have ceased to threaten.